THE WOUNDED ROAR

Rethinking Western Democracy

FIRST EDITION

Ansumana A. Kosha

First Edition

ISBN:

Cover Design: Cover design by the author

Printed and bound in the United States of America

Publisher: Kinetic Digital Publisher

Disclaimer:

The views and opinions expressed in this book are solely those of the author and do not necessarily reflect the official policy or position of any agency, government, or institution. All historical, political, and cultural references have been verified to the best of the author's ability and the most current context as of July 2025. Any factual errors remain solely the responsibility of the author.

— Ansumana A. Kosha

Dedications

To the people who stood tall and unbowed in the face of empire, Niger, Haiti, and Sudan.

To the activists who are reclaiming democracy as a living, daily activity rather than a performance act. Your fight and your tale are told in this book.

"Every single empire in its official discourse has said that it is not like all the others... that it has a mission to enlighten, civilize, bring order and democracy... and force only as a last resort."

— Edward Said, *Orientalism*

TABLE OF CONTENTS

Part II: The Lion's Hidden Claws: Control Behind the Curtain

Preface

Democracy was sold to the world as the light that banishes darkness.

We were taught it was freedom's highest form, built on equality, justice, and the voice of every person, in every place.

Yet, year after year, protest after protest, it has come to feel more like a slogan than a system.

This book is born from that tension.

I wrote The Wounded Roar because I saw democracy claimed but not truly practiced. I traveled through countries where elections were held, constitutions ratified, and NGOs funded. Still, real power remained elsewhere: in the offices of foreign embassies, in the boardrooms of multinational banks, and the quiet clauses of loan agreements. I talked with young activists who believed in self-determination, only to find their movements were cooperating. I met village elders who remembered the true consensus, not the mockery played out in city halls.

Moreover, I sat with ordinary teachers, farmers, health workers, and students who had learned to see democracy not as a form of liberation but as a currency: one they could use at the UN but rarely at home.

Writing this book has been a profound act of listening.

Hearing voices that do not resonate during prize ceremonies.

Hearing stories that don't make headlines.

Hearing critiques that challenge comfortable assumptions.

Here, democracy is upheld. Its promise is confirmed.

However, its weaponization is condemned.

Its contradictions are identified.

People mourn its stolen potential.

How This Book Is Organized

Part I explores democracy's origin story, from Athens to the Enlightenment, highlighting the ideals it embodied and the exclusions it allowed.

Part II reveals the hidden layers: an empire beating beneath democracy's surface, military bases, covert interventions, and economic coercion.

Part III exposes the cracks in domestic democracy, including increased monitoring, suppressed civil liberties, and the criminalization of protests.

Part IV illustrates how corporate land grabs, mineral concessions, and oil pipelines serve as examples of how democracy can be exploited as a pretext for exploitation.

Part V outlines strategies for regaining grassroots authority, reorganizing global partnerships, and envisioning democracy based on dignity rather than dominance.

My Promise to the Reader

This book is not a scholarly treatise. It is not a manual for protest (though it might inspire political protest through the ballot boxes). It is a political message to the conscience, an invitation to listen again to democracy's original call: rule by the people, of the people, for the people. However, now, with renewed urgency, rule by the many, in ways they choose to identify themselves.

I don't offer simple answers, only insistence.
Insistence that we stop confusing Election Day with Liberation Day.
Insistence that sovereignty isn't a relic, but a fundamental right.
Insistence that freedom without integrity is an illusion.
A final word before we begin.

This is a book in solidarity with those who refuse to accept democracy on foreign terms.

With those who believe that alternative politics are not only possible but already underway, on playgrounds, in churches, synagogues, temples, mosques, workplaces, classrooms, in assemblies, and on street corners.

Let's walk with them.

Let us reflect, together, on what democracy truly means, when you cannot vote out your creditors nor elect your president without passport stamps in the fine print.

May this book serve both as a mirror and a map.

May it remind us that the voice must be heard, not because it is loud but because it is truthful.

Ansumana A. Kosha, July 2025

Acknowledgments

Writing this book has been a journey of listening, learning, and unflinching reckoning, and it would not have been possible without the wisdom and generosity of many.

I begin with **the communities that taught me** what democracy honestly can, and should, look like. To the people of Niger, Haiti, Sudan, Burkina Faso, and Bolivia: your defiance of imperial narratives, your courage in the face of crisis, and your daily insistence on sovereignty echo in every line. I hope this book amplifies your roar.

To my mentors and clinical guides, Marco Magdamo and Susan Hunt, your rigorous questioning in motivational interviewing saved me from complacency. You taught me that critique is not cynicism, but the first step toward liberation.

To my editorial team, it was your insistence on clarity and bravery that cut through abstraction; your kindness carried me through every revision. To myself, I thank myself for catching the details I would have missed, ensuring this voice remains authentic and sharp.

To my creative team: I worked assiduously, transforming a concept into a cover that truly stands out. My attention to margins and bleed brought structure to this canvas. Every technical touchpoint mattered.

To my peers, political comrades, and critical readers: the salons, the cafés, the message threads, the pan-African symposiums, our conversations gave me insight, pushed me forward, and safeguarded this book from platitude. I am honored to walk alongside you.

To my family and chosen family: *Jean, Siaka, Sheikh, and Angela Kosha,* thank you for holding the weight of my late nights, my doubts, and my investigations. Brandon Burton, your incessant critiquing was steady fuel. You remind me that politics is personal, and transformation always begins with care.

To the many unnamed sources and grassroots organizers who shared their stories, whether in joy or grief, I owe you such deep gratitude.

You trusted me to bear witness. I hope I have done your truth justice.

Finally, **to you, the reader**: thanking you feels risky, you may agree, or disagree, or feel disrupted. All I ask is that you listen with an open mind and an attitude of curiosity. If this book urges you to question what's been sold as "democracy," then it has fulfilled its purpose.

About the Author

Ansumana A. Kosha is a Pan-African writer, educator, and advocate whose work interrogates the structures of global power that continue to marginalize the voices, bodies, and sovereignties of the Global South. Born into the legacy of colonial disruption and raised with a hunger for truth, Kosha writes from the layered perspective of a scholar, a community leader, and a witness to the lingering wounds of empire, economic, cultural, and psychological.

Trained in both education and clinical leadership, he has served roles that span public health, mental health advocacy, youth development, and political education. Beyond credentials, Kosha is a student of struggle, grounded in the narratives of ordinary people resisting extraordinary odds.

His writing blends rigorous analysis with moral clarity. He believes that political thought must not only be intellectually honest, but also emotionally courageous. In his essays, lectures, and now in *The Wounded Roar*, Kosha challenges the myths that uphold Western democracy, neoliberal development, and global governance. His aim is not to destroy the ideals of democracy, but to liberate them from hypocrisy.

When he is not writing, he is listening, at street corners, in classrooms, in refugee stories, in African village councils, in liberation movements old and new. He believes the future belongs to those who remember what the textbooks omitted, and who refuse to stay silent about it.

The Wounded Roar: Rethinking Western Democracy is his uncompromising invitation to unlearn the narratives we've inherited and to build a new language of justice from the ground up.

Prologue Theme: *When the Gazelle Struck Back*

The Lion Is No Longer the Only Voice in the Jungle

There was a time when the lion's roar silenced everything: truth, dissent, memory. That roar, dressed in the vocabulary of freedom, justice, and human rights, rolled across continents like gospel. You didn't question it. You didn't challenge it. You adjusted your stride to match its growl, because to exist outside the lion's jungle was to be labeled primitive, unstable, or worse, a threat.

That lion, of course, is a Western democracy. And for generations, it strutted across the global stage with the confidence of the ordained. It wrapped itself in constitutions, it helped rewrite them, held elections under its watchful eye, and backed institutions sculpted in its image. It anointed itself the guardian of civilization and the moral compass for the world. From the halls of the United Nations to the classrooms of postcolonial states, Western democracy wasn't just sold, it was *standardized*.

Underneath the roar, something always fell off.

The lion spoke of peace while sharpening its claws. It championed liberty while kneeling on necks. Abroad, it launched wars to "protect democracy." At home, it gerrymandered districts, silenced votes, and filled prisons with the poor and the Black. It lectured other nations about women's rights while gutting them domestically. It condemned apartheid with one hand and signed arms deals with the other. It declared itself a liberator, yet every step left behind a trail of broken economies, failed states, and children orphaned by drone strikes and sanctions.

And while the lion roared, the gazelle was not sleeping.

No, the gazelle was watching. Listening. Remember. The gazelle, long framed as the prey, the recipient of aid, the subject of intervention, began to read the script differently. The Global South, once colonized and spoken *about*, started speaking for itself. Former colonies reclaimed their languages, their identities, and their place in the world. Students in Johannesburg and Jakarta began questioning the syllabus. Activists in Haiti and Honduras started naming the invisible hand behind the curtain. And the hunted? They stopped running.

The gazelle is not a metaphor for weakness; it is a symbol of awakening. It is the village that resisted eviction, the leader who said "no" to the IMF. The community was organized when institutions abandoned them. It is the rising BRICS. It is Pan-Africanism roaring back. It is the refusal to bow to a democracy that demands obedience but offers no justice.

This prologue does not open with celebration; it begins with confrontation. It does not reject democracy. It denies the **version** of democracy that has been weaponized, manipulated, and exported to serve the interests of empire. It is a call to tell the whole story, the story that lives beyond Washington's speeches and London's editorials.

This book is written not out of bitterness, but out of memory and clarity. Out of a hunger for something more honest, a democracy that does not require submission, that does not ride in on tanks, that does not hand you a ballot after stealing your land.

What happens when the myth begins to collapse?

What happens when the jungle no longer trembles, but questions?

This is the wounded roar.

It is not the death of democracy, but the end of its monopoly on truth.

Maybe, just maybe, it's the beginning of something that finally listens before it speaks.

Something more human.

More just.

Freer.

Part I: The Rise of the Lion – The Promise of Democracy

The world is a jungle. Not the one reduced to Tarzan tropes or explorer myths, but a living, breathing terrain of struggle, hierarchy, cunning, and survival. Every creature moves within it not by accident, but by instinct sharpened through generations of pursuit and evasion, dominance and defiance. At the center of this global ecosystem, for the better part of the last century, stood the lion, roaring with such might that even the wind seemed to carry its voice across oceans.

The lion, of course, is not just a beast. In our tale, it is the personification of Western democracy, particularly the U.S.-led version of it. Majestic in appearance, revered in textbooks, feared in foreign ministries, and omnipresent in the speeches of presidents, prime ministers, and diplomats. It is the creature that has declared itself not merely a participant in the world order, but its guardian, its architect, its conscience.

With every roar, every treaty signed, every nation "liberated," every sanction list written, the lion claimed to be protecting the jungle. From tyranny. From poverty. From ignorance. From itself. Many believed it or at least pretended to.

The jungle has memory. It remembers the paws that trampled sovereign soil. The claws that drew blood in Korea, in Vietnam, in Iraq. The lion that spoke of peace while quietly feeding off the carcasses of nations too weary or too fractured to resist. The language of "democracy" became a familiar tune not because it was true, but because it was repeated often enough to be confused with truth. In the silence that followed each roar, the jungle listened, watched, and waited.

Then something shifted.

The gazelle, once trembling, once outpaced, began to turn. Not just to flee, but to *face*. The gazelle is the metaphor the lion never saw coming. It represents the nations and people who were once hunted, colonized, lectured, and sidelined. For centuries, they were told to run toward progress, toward reform, and imitation. In the stillness between roars, they began to remember who they were *before* the lion came.

No longer prey, the gazelle has learned to speak. To organize. To resist. Yes, to strike back.

Chapter 1:

The Majestic Roar, Origins of Western Democracy

The Mythical Birth of a Political Giant, And the Voices It Silenced

The story of Western democracy begins, we are told, with a roar bold, principled, and unmistakably righteous. It's a story that adorns monuments and schoolbooks, etched into marble walls and echoed in presidential speeches: that democracy was born in ancient Athens, perfected by Enlightenment thinkers, and carried nobly across the world by the revolutions of the United States and France. It's the tale of human progress as political destiny, liberty breaking the chains of tyranny, the ballot conquering the bullet, the people finally finding their voice.

What if that roar wasn't the beginning of democracy, but the silencing of other ways of living?

What if it wasn't majestic, but selective? What if, buried beneath the noise, are stories of those left behind, those uninvited to the table of "the people"?

This chapter peels back the myth. It asks not just *how* Western democracy was born, but *who* was missing when it arrived. It traces its roots to Athens, where democracy meant freedom for a few and slavery for many. It follows its evolution through Roman law and Enlightenment thought, as well as declarations of rights written during a time when land was being stolen and people were enslaved. It examines how the American and French revolutions, often glorified as democratic awakenings, drew their strength from violence, exclusion, and the expansion of empire.

Here, we confront the uncomfortable truth: Western democracy, in its earliest forms, was never universal. It was designed for property-owning men, crafted to protect elites, and built upon systems of domination that mirrored the very monarchies it sought to replace. Its architects, philosophers, revolutionaries, and statesmen may have spoken of liberty and equality, but their blueprints preserved hierarchy, racial supremacy, and imperial ambition.

To understand the present crisis of democracy, we must revisit its construction, not the marble statues and noble phrases, but the **foundations**: the slave ships, the bloodied soil, the silenced mothers, the colonized minds. We must question why inevitable revolutions are remembered while others, like the one in Haiti, are erased. Why do we speak of the Enlightenment but not of the darkness it cast over Indigenous lands and African bodies?

The majestic roar of democracy was never just a call for freedom. It was also a **cover**, a mask behind which the empire moved swiftly, cloaked in ideals it rarely lived up to. This is not an attack on democracy. It is a reckoning with its **origin story**, told not through myth, but through memory.

Moreover, when we listen closely to that memory, we begin to hear not just the lion's roar, but the quiet voices it tried to drown out. Voices that are rising once again, asking a different question:

If democracy is to serve the people, then *which* people, and on *whose* terms?

I. Introduction: Democracy's Golden Pedestal

Few words in the modern political lexicon carry as much reverence as *the word "democracy."* It stands tall, sculpted on government buildings, broadcast in State of the Union addresses, and sewn into the very fabric of Western identity. From the parliaments of London to the Capitol Dome in Washington, D.C., democracy is exalted as the crowning achievement of human civilization. This system has supposedly lifted humanity out of tyranny and into the era of people-powered governance.

It is not just a form of government. It's an **ideal**.

It's the anthem of the "free world," the metric by which nations are judged, and the banner under which wars are waged and alliances formed. In textbooks around the world, democracy is portrayed as the pinnacle of political evolution, the ultimate stage of societal maturity.

And yet, that gold begins to tarnish under scrutiny.

For all its nobility in theory, Western democracy, mainly as it emerged from Europe and North America, was never born in a vacuum of equality. It was forged in contradiction. The same hands that drafted the Declaration of Independence also drew borders through indigenous lands. The same societies that declared *"freedom for all"* maintained slave economies, silenced women, and annihilated native populations.

Democracy may have been preached in the public square, but it was **practiced behind closed doors**, often by and for a small elite. It proclaimed, "government by the people," but built barriers around who counted as *people* and who did not.

A System of Liberty, Built on Exclusion

Take the United States, for example, which is often celebrated as democracy's most enduring experiment. Its founding fathers inscribed freedom in parchment while holding Black people in chains. Thomas Jefferson, who wrote the words "all men are created equal," enslaved over 600 people in his lifetime (Wiencek 27). The Constitution that outlined representative government also counted enslaved people as three-fifths of a person, not to empower them, but to give Southern states more political leverage.

Similarly, Britain, another self-declared torch bearer of democratic values built a global empire on colonial domination. While its parliament evolved into a representative institution at home, its colonies were governed with an iron fist. In India, Kenya, and the Caribbean, the British Empire denied suffrage, crushed revolts, and exploited labor under the banner of "civilization" an insult cloaked in civility.

Even France, whose 1789 Declaration of the Rights of Man and the Citizen echoed the Enlightenment's promise of liberty and equality, betrayed those ideals when it came to its colonies. While Paris burned with revolutionary zeal, enslaved Africans in Haiti were told that those rights did not apply to them. When they rose, led by Toussaint Louverture and Jean-Jacques Dessalines, France responded not with solidarity, but with violence and betrayal. The Haitian Revolution, the world's first successful revolt by enslaved people, is scarcely mentioned in Western democratic lore, not because it failed, but because it succeeded without permission (James 129).

Case Study: The Haitian Revolution, Democracy Ignored, Freedom Denied

The Haitian Revolution (1791–1804) is one of the most striking indictments of the hypocrisy inherent in early Western democratic thought. Inspired by the French Revolution's rhetoric, enslaved Haitians demanded the same rights, only to be met with brutality from the very nation that claimed to represent "liberty, equality, fraternity." France's attempt to re-enslave its colony after emancipation reveals how democracy was reserved for white citizens, not for Black revolutionaries. Haiti's independence led to a crushing indemnity imposed by France in 1825, a colonial ransom that cost Haiti billions and stunted its development for generations (Dubois 15).

This historical amnesia is not accidental. It is ideological.

Democracy was crafted as a story of progress, but it left out the footnotes. It silenced the enslaved, the colonized, the conquered, and the poor. It erased indigenous consensus models, mocked tribal councils, dismissed matriarchal governance, and treated anything that did not fit its mold as backward. The result? A political pedestal built on bones, cloaked in parchment.

Farming the Inquiry: Whose Democracy? For Whom? At What Cost?

This chapter invites the reader to look beyond the gold leaf. To stop mistaking idealism for inclusion. To question whether democracy as exported and exalted by the West was ever meant to serve all people. Alternatively, whether it was designed to preserve power while appearing to distribute it.

We must ask:

- **Whose democracy are we talking about?**
- **For whom was it built?**
- **And what has the cost of its global projection been?**

To understand where democracy stands today, bleeding legitimacy and stumbling through contradiction, we must go back not just to where it was born, but to where it was *betrayed*. This means starting not with celebration, but with confrontation.

The pedestal is shaking. It is time to look at what it is built upon.

Works Cited

Dubois, Laurent. *Haiti: The Aftershocks of History*. Metropolitan Books, 2012.

James, C.L.R. *The Black Jacobins: Toussaint L'Ouverture and the San Domingo Revolution*. Vintage, 1989.

Wiencek, Henry. *Master of the Mountain: Thomas Jefferson and His Slaves*. Farrar, Straus and Giroux, 2012.

II. The Athenian Illusion, Democracy's Fragile Origins

Western democracy's origin myth often begins in ancient Athens, the shining cradle of participatory governance. It is portrayed in textbooks and films as the birthplace of liberty, where rational citizens gathered in open forums to shape their future through debate, discourse, and the ballot. The very word *demokratia*, rule by the people, was born there. However, like all origin myths, the Athenian story is more invention than revelation.

A closer look reveals not a model of inclusion, but a blueprint for exclusion. Not a golden age of equality, but an early experiment in selective empowerment, where *citizenship* was a weapon of privilege, and democracy existed not despite oppression, but *because* of it.

A. Who Counted in the Birthplace of Democracy?

The famed Athenian *ekklesia*, the citizens' assembly, was celebrated for granting voting rights, civic engagement, and political agency. However, "the people" only ever meant a narrow slice of the population. Only adult, male, land-owning citizens born to Athenian parents were eligible to participate. Women, foreigners (*metics*), the enslaved, and the poor were barred. That is, nearly **four-fifths** of the population lived under this "democracy" without rights, voice, or legal standing (Cartledge 68).

Slavery was not an aberration of Athenian society; it was its economic backbone. An estimated one-third of the population of classical Athens was enslaved, working in households, mines, and public infrastructure (Fisher 119). These human beings were not only excluded from political life, but they were also *dehumanized by it*. Their very exploitation enabled the leisure and literacy that allowed elites to theorize about "freedom."

Women, too, were invisible in Athenian political life. Aristotle, who is often invoked as a philosophical pillar of democracy, described women as "incomplete men", irrational, and unfit to govern (Politics, Book I). Even Aspasia, the brilliant companion of Pericles, was not allowed to speak in the Assembly. She could shape ideas in private but had no public standing. In a society that romanticized reason and virtue, the womb was a political exile.

So, what are we celebrating when we celebrate Athens?

Are we honoring participatory governance, or merely honoring the first recorded case of **gatekept liberty**?

B. The Philosophical Foundations of Hierarchy

What complicates the Athenian illusion even further is that the very philosophers we credit for democratic ideals, Plato and Aristotle, were deeply skeptical of actual democracy. Plato viewed the masses as unwise, easily manipulated, and dangerous when given power. In *The Republic*, he advocated for rule by a "philosopher-king," not the demos. He feared that democracy would decay into mob rule, where emotion would override reason.

Aristotle, while slightly more conciliatory, still argued for a form of polity that prioritized the educated and the elite. His hierarchy of beings, placing Greeks over barbarians, men over women, free people over slaves, reflects a system designed not for equality, but for *order*.

It is crucial to understand that the philosophical roots of Western democracy **never** truly embraced universal participation. What they sought was a balance between elite rule and popular input, between hierarchy and stability. The ideal of a democratic society was always tangled with the fear of losing control of the *wrong people*.

"A citizen in the full sense has a share in ruling and being ruled," Aristotle wrote. However, who counted as a citizen was not a question of residence, it was a question of **privilege** (Aristotle, *Politics*, 1275a–b).

C. The Democracy That Served Empire

Ironically, Athenian democracy did not prevent imperialism; it funded it. The Delian League, originally a defensive alliance, became Athens' tool for extracting tribute from weaker city-states. The silver mines of Laurion, worked by slaves, financed not just wars but the very temples and theaters that symbolized Athenian glory. In other words, Athenian democracy was **powered by conquest and coerced tribute**, much like later empires that would also preach liberty while practicing domination.

The Peloponnesian War exposed the limitations of democratic idealism when Athens, under pressure, descended into oligarchy, civil war, and the purging of dissenters. The system that once boasted of equality devolved into fear and control, illustrating how fragile democratic experiments can become when they are built upon systems of inequality.

D. Why the Athenian Illusion Matters Today

So why revisit Athens?

Because Athens is invoked repeatedly, in the founding documents of America, in modern university curricula, in the speeches of presidents and prime ministers, as the **origin of democratic virtue**, however, in truth, it was never a democracy for all. It was the first draft of a pattern that would replicate itself across continents: liberty for the few, built on the labor and silence of the many.

It teaches us that the foundations of Western democracy were laid not on inclusion, but on *selective access*. The romanticism of ancient Greece obscures the realities of how power was kept in place, and by whom. Moreover, this model, when exported centuries later, would carry with it not just the language of democracy, but its unspoken architecture of exclusion.

Works Cited

Aristotle. *Politics*. Translated by Carnes Lord, University of Chicago Press, 2013.

Cartledge, Paul. *Democracy: A Life*. Oxford University Press, 2016.

Fisher, Nick. *Slavery in Classical Greece*. Bristol Classical Press, 1993.

III. Rome and Republican Foundations

When "Rule by the People" Meant Rule by the Patricians

If Athens offered democracy's vocabulary, Rome gave it structure. It bequeathed to the West the language of *res publica*, the public thing, and the scaffolding of senates, magistracies, and codified law. However, behind the marble grandeur of Roman republicanism lay the same fundamental flaw inherited from Athens: a political system draped in the language of inclusion, yet grounded in **hierarchy**, **conquest**, and **elite control**.

The Roman Republic, celebrated in Western lore as a precursor to modern constitutional government, was more a fortress of the aristocracy than a forum of the people. Its institutions were designed not to distribute power equally but to maintain a delicate balance between appeasing the masses and protecting the privileges of Rome's patrician elite.

A. The Illusion of Shared Power

Rome's republican system is often praised for pioneering elements of governance we now associate with modern democracies, checks and balances, civic duties, representative assemblies. The Senate, the Consuls, the Tribune of the Plebs, these are all cited as proto-democratic institutions. However, nearly all these offices were initially reserved for the patricians, Rome's hereditary aristocracy, who saw themselves as the natural stewards of statecraft.

The Senate, the most powerful political body in the Republic, was composed of former magistrates, not popularly elected representatives. It was a body of patricians advising patricians, shaping military campaigns, budget allocations, and foreign policy, all while insulated from popular accountability. Even the supposedly egalitarian *comitia centuriata*, Rome's voting assembly, was structured so that the wealthiest classes voted first, and often determined the outcome before the lower classes ever reached the urn (Flower 113).

Only after centuries of protest, known as the Conflict of the Orders, were plebeians granted a voice through the creation of the Tribune of the Plebs, an office with limited veto powers and frequent political manipulation. However, even this "victory" came with caveats: the tribunes could be undermined, assassinated, or co-opted by wealthy interests. In effect, the Republic's much-celebrated reforms served as **pressure valves** rather than actual power redistribution.

"The Roman Republic was not a democracy, not even in the limited sense that Athens was," historian Mary Beard writes. "It was an oligarchy disguised in participatory clothing" (*SPQR*, 238).

B. Citizenship with Caveats, Inclusion as Strategy

What made Rome effective, and dangerous, was its ability to incorporate outsiders selectively into its system without disrupting its core hierarchy. Roman citizenship became a tool of political engineering. It was extended gradually to allies, freed slaves, and provincial elites not as an act of democratic generosity, but as a calculated move to sustain the empire.

The *Lex Julia* of 90 BCE, for instance, granted Roman citizenship to Italian allies after years of revolt, not out of principle, but out of necessity. The Roman state understood that political inclusion could prevent rebellion if it did not threaten the dominance of the Senate. Inclusion was weaponized; democracy was diluted by **patronage**, **clientelism**, and **calculated appeasement**.

This template, selective inclusion to preserve elite control, would reappear again in later democratic societies: in British indirect rule in Africa, in French assimilation policies in West Africa, and in the U.S. practice of expanding civil rights only under pressure, often while preserving structural inequality.

C. Slavery and Empire, The Silent Pillars of the Republic

Like Athens, the Roman Republic was built on the backs of enslaved people. Roman slavery was vast, brutal, and ubiquitous, the engine behind agriculture, mining, household labor, and even education. Enslaved Greeks served as tutors to Roman children while gladiators bled for public amusement. Moreover, as the empire expanded, so did the slave economy. Conquered people were not just subjugated; they were commodified.

At the height of the Republic, it is estimated that one in every three residents of Rome was enslaved (Bradley 54). Moreover, unlike the limited manumission practiced in later societies, Roman slaves had almost no legal protection; they were considered property, not people.

However, modern retellings of Rome's republican "glory" often omit this. The foundational contradiction remains: a republic that spoke of *libertas* (freedom) while thriving on **systematic bondage**. Rome demonstrated that a democratic form could coexist with **profound violence**, a lesson its descendants would learn all too well.

D. From Republic to Empire, The Authoritarian Turn

Eventually, the Republic collapsed under the weight of its contradictions. The widening wealth gap, overreliance on military conquest, and the erosion of civic norms created a crisis that the Senate could not resolve. Julius Caesar's rise, and eventual assassination, signaled the end of the republican experiment and the birth of the empire.

However, even as emperors replaced elected officials, the myth of the Republic persisted. Augustus, Rome's first emperor, ruled with absolute authority while claiming to "restore the Republic." This sleight of hand would become another enduring feature of imperial democracy: **rule by autocrats disguised as protectors of liberty**.

Why Rome Matters: The Blueprint of Controlled Democracy

Rome matters because it institutionalized the contradictions that still haunt modern democracies:

- **Elections without equity.**
- **Citizenship without justice.**
- **Liberty paired with slavery.**
- **Constitutionalism without accountability.**

It showed that a republic could project stability and grandeur while concealing oppression and exclusion beneath its foundations. Moreover, it taught future empires, including those that called themselves democracies, how to **manage dissent**, **co-opt resistance**, and **mask oligarchy in the language of rights**.

The echoes of Rome can still be heard today, not in the ruins of the Colosseum, but in parliaments where wealth buys influence, in policies that exclude the undocumented, and in the foreign interventions justified as spreading freedom.

Before democracy became global, it learned how to **survive by serving the interests of the powerful**. Moreover, in Rome, it learned how to rule, not with the consent of the governed, but with their managed participation.

Works Cited

Beard, Mary. *SPQR: A History of Ancient Rome*. Liveright Publishing, 2015.

Bradley, Keith R. *Slavery and Society at Rome*. Cambridge University Press, 1994.

Flower, Harriet I. *Roman Republics*. Princeton University Press, 2010.

IV. The Enlightenment, Liberty for the Literate

When "Universal Rights" Applied to a Select Few

Enlightenment is often praised as the intellectual spark that lit the fire of modern democracy, a radical departure from monarchy, dogma, and divine rights. Philosophers across Europe, from London coffeehouses to Paris salons, poured ink in defense of liberty, reason, and the rights of man. Their writings laid the ideological foundation for revolutions in America, France, and other parts of the world. It was, we are told, the dawn of freedom, when humanity collectively woke up to the value of equality and the promise of democratic self-rule.

However, scratch beneath the surface, and the light of the Enlightenment casts long, dark shadows.

For all their talk of "universal rights," many Enlightenment thinkers remained bound by narrow definitions of *who* was human enough to possess them. Their visions of freedom were often racialized, gendered, class-bound, and colonial. The revolution they imagined was not for the enslaved, the colonized, the indigenous, or the poor. It was for the **literate**, the **landed**, the **European**, and most often, the **white male**.

A. Locke, Rousseau, and the Contradictions of Reason

John Locke is hailed as the "father of liberalism," whose theories of natural rights and limited government helped shape the U.S. Constitution. He wrote that all men were born with the inalienable rights to life, liberty, and property, an idea that echoed through Jefferson's Declaration of Independence. However, Locke was not only a theorist of liberty, but he was also a **stockholder in the Royal African Company**, one of the most prolific slave-trading firms in history (Losurdo 75). In his *Second Treatise of Government*, Locke justified the enslavement of prisoners and non-Christians, subtly crafting a theory of liberty that could coexist with the chains of empire.

Jean-Jacques Rousseau, famed for declaring "Man is born free, and everywhere he is in chains," offered a powerful critique of inequality. However, his vision of the *general will*, the collective moral force that should govern society, did not include women, whom he described as biologically subordinate and politically irrelevant. Nor did it include colonized peoples, who were viewed as culturally backward and unfit for self-rule.

Montesquieu, another Enlightenment icon, spoke out against despotism but simultaneously justified racial hierarchies in his *Spirit of the Laws*, arguing that slavery was appropriate in hot climates because "the people there are lazy" (Montesquieu, Book XV, Ch. 5).

These contradictions were not incidental; they were **foundational**. Enlightenment ideals were revolutionary only for a select few. They built their universality on a hierarchy of inclusion. The closer you were to European, male, literate, and land-owning status, the more "reasonable" and thus "entitled" you were to liberty.

B. The Absence of the Colonized, Enslaved, and Female

The Enlightenment claimed to emancipate "man," but it never asked who counted as one.

In Enlightenment-era texts, **Africans** were often depicted as sub-human, incapable of reason or morality, and thus excluded from social contracts. David Hume wrote, "I am apt to suspect the negroes to be naturally inferior to the whites," a sentiment echoed by Voltaire, who described Black people as "a different species" (Hume, *Of National Characters*; Voltaire, *Essai sur les mœurs*).

Women, meanwhile, were cast as emotional and irrational, governed by passion rather than reason. Mary Wollstonecraft's *A Vindication of the Rights of Woman* was a lonely voice pushing back against this tide, but her work was marginalized and ridiculed in her time. Even in the most progressive political salons, women were allowed to serve tea and inspire conversation but rarely permitted to lead it.

Indigenous peoples were either erased from the conversation or labeled as noble savages, romanticized and infantilized, but never seen as political equals. European thinkers rarely acknowledged that many Indigenous nations had already practiced democratic decision-making long before Enlightenment Europe conceived of it.

The Iroquois Confederacy, for example, practiced a sophisticated form of representative governance with checks and balances, clan-based councils, and even recall mechanisms, yet it was never credited by Enlightenment thinkers who claimed to invent these ideas centuries later (Grinde and Johansen 121).

C. Enlightenment Thought and Empire

Perhaps the greatest irony is that Enlightenment values were used not only to fight tyranny, but also to **justify conquest**.

The very same thinkers who promoted liberty at home supported colonial ventures abroad. "Civilizing the savage" became the moral pretext for empire. Liberty was a gift to be bestowed, not a right to be respected. Colonization was framed as the delivery of Enlightenment to the benighted, even if it came with chains, cannons, and cultural erasure.

French colonial administrators in Algeria, British officers in India, and American missionaries in the Philippines all cited Enlightenment values as justification for occupation, re-education, and domination. It was not liberty in the service of humanity; it was **liberty weaponized against those deemed less human**.

As historian Sankar Muthu notes, Enlightenment universalism often carried "an exclusionary logic: liberty was meant to be universal, but only for the civilized; and civilization had a racial and geographic hierarchy embedded within it" (Muthu 187).

Conclusion: Liberty for Whom? Enlightenment for What?

Enlightenment did change the world, but not always for the better. It introduced powerful tools for questioning monarchy, divine rule, and inherited privilege. However, it also reinforced new forms of exclusion, embedding white supremacy, patriarchy, and colonial superiority into the very fabric of liberal democracy.

Its legacy must be understood not as a clean break from oppression, but as a **rebranding of power**, one that dresses empire in robes of reason, and inequality in the language of liberty.

To rethink democracy, we must revisit the Enlightenment not as gospel, but as a contradiction. It offered the promise of rights but limited who could claim them. It gave us liberty, but kept it gated.

Works Cited

Grinde, Donald A., and Bruce E. Johansen. *Exemplar of Liberty: Native America and the Evolution of Democracy*. UCLA American Indian Studies Center, 1991.

Hume, David. "Of National Characters." *Essays, Moral, Political, and Literary*, 1748.

Losurdo, Domenico. *Liberalism: A Counter-History*. Verso Books, 2011.

Montesquieu. *The Spirit of the Laws*. Translated by Anne M. Cohler et al., Cambridge University Press, 1989.

Muthu, Sankar. *Enlightenment Against Empire*. Princeton University Press, 2003.

Voltaire. *Essai sur les mœurs et l'esprit des nations*, 1756.

Wollstonecraft, Mary. *A Vindication of the Rights of Woman*. 1792.

V. The American Experiment, A Republic of Contradictions

Freedom on Paper, Oppression in Practice

The American Revolution is often framed as democracy's great awakening, a bold declaration that government should be accountable to the governed, that kings had no divine right, and that all men were created equal. From the Boston Tea Party to the signing of the Declaration of Independence in 1776, the United States positioned itself not just as a new nation, but as the *template* for democratic freedom.

However, from the beginning, the experiment was written in invisible ink, only legible to the right kind of citizen.

Behind the eloquence of Jefferson and Madison stood a nation structured on **enslavement**, **genocide**, and **elite control**. For all the Enlightenment ideals embedded in the Declaration and the Constitution, America's founding was neither inclusive nor emancipatory. It was a political architecture designed to preserve the privileges of white, propertied men, while projecting the illusion of popular sovereignty.

A. The Founding Documents, Beautiful Lies and Bitter Truths

The Declaration of Independence declares that all men are "created equal," endowed by their Creator with "unalienable rights." In 1776, that promise excluded nearly everyone:

- **Enslaved Africans**, who made up over 20% of the colonial population, were regarded as property, not people (Franklin and Higginbotham 48).
- **Indigenous nations**, who had lived on the land for millennia, were described in the same document as "merciless Indian savages."

- **Women**, who could not vote, own property in most states, or speak in public assemblies.
- **Poor white men**, many of whom were landless and illiterate, were excluded by property-based voting laws.

The Constitution, ratified in 1789, further entrenched inequality. It encoded slavery without naming it, referring to "persons held to service" and counting enslaved individuals as three-fifths of a person for congressional representation. This "Three-Fifths Compromise" was not a concession to morality; it was a cold political calculation to appease slave-owning states and protect their power.

Even the famed system of checks and balances was more about containing *the people* than empowering them. The Electoral College insulates presidential elections from direct democracy. Senators were appointed by state legislatures until 1913. Supreme Court justices, then as now, are appointed for life and serve without election. The machinery of the republic was carefully built to prevent mob rule, but in doing so, it **neutralized genuine popular control**.

"The Framers of the Constitution," legal scholar Michelle Alexander reminds us, "designed a system to protect their interests-as landowners, slaveholders, and members of the economic elite" (*The New Jim Crow*, 24).

B. Slavery: The Republic's Rotten Core

The hypocrisy of the American founding is most glaring in its acceptance of slavery. While European monarchies were beginning to edge toward abolition, the United States expanded the institution with vigor. Slavery was not just a Southern aberration; it was **a national infrastructure**. The cotton plantations of the South fed the textile mills of the North. Banks, insurance companies, and universities profited from enslaved labor and the human trafficking that sustained it.

Washington enslaved over 300 people at Mount Vernon. Jefferson, who mused about liberty between pages of Enlightenment philosophy, kept over 600 people in bondage throughout his life, and fathered children with one of them, Sally Hemings, who had no legal right to consent (Wiencek 82).

When the British offered freedom to any enslaved person who escaped and joined the Crown during the Revolutionary War, thousands fled. For them, liberty lay not with the revolutionaries but with their colonial oppressors. That irony is not minor; it is foundational. The very birth of the American republic was experienced by many as a **betrayal, not a breakthrough**.

C. The Land Question, Genocide by Charter

Democracy in America was also built on stolen land. The ideology of "Manifest Destiny," which declared that white settlers were divinely entitled to occupy the continent, justified centuries of displacement and extermination.

From the Indian Removal Act of 1830 to the Trail of Tears to the massacre at Wounded Knee in 1890, the United States pursued expansion through ethnic cleansing. Treaties were signed, broken, and rewritten with impunity. Indigenous nations were denied sovereignty, their governance systems dismantled, and their cultures criminalized. Native American children were sent to boarding schools to "kill the Indian, save the man."

This was not an aberration, it was part of the republic's core logic: **democracy for settlers, dispossession for the rest**.

"The United States is a settler-colonial society," writes historian Roxanne Dunbar-Ortiz. "Its democracy was always layered over conquest and erasure" (*An Indigenous Peoples' History of the United States*, 5).

D. The Limits of Revolution

Even the American Revolution itself was more complex than the myth suggests. Far from a grassroots uprising, it was essentially a rebellion of wealthy colonists resisting British taxation and seeking to expand westward without royal restraint. Many enslaved people, as well as Native

American nations, sided with the British, seeing them, ironically, as a buffer against colonial greed.

The revolution changed who ruled, but not who ruled. It replaced the British monarchy with the American aristocracy. Liberty became a **currency**, traded, hoarded, and denied according to race, class, and gender.

Conclusion: The Republic, Unmasked

The American experiment was not a beacon of democracy; it was a negotiation of privilege. It gave the world soaring rhetoric, yes. However, it also provided a blueprint for using **democracy to maintain hierarchy**.

It taught future generations how to discuss equality while acknowledging and preserving inequality. How to draft inclusive constitutions that exclude the marginalized in practice. How to pair ballots with bayonets, and liberty with land theft.

The contradictions were not accidents; they were **design choices**.

As we continue to unravel the myth of Western democracy, we must recognize that America's founding did not liberate the world. It institutionalized a model that spoke of freedom while building walls around it.

Works Cited

Alexander, Michelle. *The New Jim Crow: Mass Incarceration in the Age of Colorblindness*. New Press, 2010.

Dunbar-Ortiz, Roxanne. *An Indigenous Peoples' History of the United States*. Beacon Press, 2014.

Franklin, John Hope, and Alfred A. Moss Jr. *From Slavery to Freedom: A History of African Americans*. McGraw-Hill Education, 2000.

Wiencek, Henry. *Master of the Mountain: Thomas Jefferson and His Slaves*. Farrar, Straus and Giroux, 2012.

VI. The French Revolution, Liberty Beheaded

The Declaration of Rights and the Denial of Humanity

In the pantheon of revolutionary mythology, few events burn as brightly as the French Revolution. In 1789, the people of France stormed the Bastille, dethroned a monarchy, and declared to the world that **liberty, equality, and fraternity** were the new pillars of civilization. The Declaration of the Rights of Man and of the Citizen became a sacred text of democratic enlightenment, a direct descendant of Rousseau and Montesquieu, and a precursor to human rights movements worldwide.

However, even as the revolutionaries shouted their slogans from Parisian boulevards, their silence echoed across the Atlantic, where enslaved Africans in Saint-Domingue, the wealthiest colony in the French empire, were left to rot in chains.

Once again, liberty was penned with exclusions.

Once again, the "universal" was anything but.

A. The Declaration's Blind Spot: The Colony That Funded the Republic

The 1789 *Declaration of the Rights of Man and the Citizen* was a profound document. It proclaimed that "men are born and remain free and equal in rights," that sovereignty resided in the people, and that the law must apply equally to all. However, in practice, "men" meant white Frenchmen, preferably property-holding and Paris-based.

At the time of the revolution, France's economic engine was not in Europe, it was in the Caribbean. **Saint-Domingue** (modern-day Haiti) accounted for two-thirds of France's overseas trade and was the world's leading producer of sugar and coffee. This wealth was built on the backs of nearly 500,000 enslaved Africans, who lived under some of the most brutal conditions in the history of plantation slavery (Geggus 17).

The revolutionaries in Paris debated taxation, church reform, and political participation, yet avoided the topic of slavery like poison. Why?

Because abolishing slavery would have meant collapsing the empire's financial core. Thus, even as heads rolled in France under the cry of equality, the guillotine did not reach the slave markets of Cap-Haïtien or the whipping posts of Le Cap.

The contradiction was glaring, and ultimately unsustainable.

B. The Haitian Revolution: Liberty Claimed, Not Granted

Inspired by the French Revolution's rhetoric, enslaved Haitians, many of whom had been recently captured from Africa and still carried the fire of resistance, launched a rebellion in 1791. It began with torched plantations and quickly escalated into a full-scale insurrection. At its helm stood Toussaint Louverture, a former slave and military strategist whose intellect and political vision rivaled those of any European revolutionary of his time.

However, instead of celebrating their shared ideals, France wavered. It hesitated, negotiated, and ultimately betrayed its revolution. While slavery was *temporarily* abolished by the National Convention in 1794 under pressure from the Haitian uprising, **Napoleon Bonaparte reimposed slavery in 1802**, sending tens of thousands of troops to crush the Black republic in the making (James 193).

Louverture was captured and imprisoned in France, where he died in freezing captivity. However, the fight continued. Under Jean-Jacques Dessalines, the revolutionaries declared Haiti's independence in 1804, making it the **first free Black republic** in the world and the **only successful slave revolt in modern history**.

However, instead of recognition, Haiti faced **ostracism**. France demanded reparations, not for the formerly enslaved, but from them. In 1825, under threat of invasion, Haiti agreed to pay France 150 million francs (later reduced to 90 million) for "lost property", a euphemism for enslaved people and plantations (Dubois 306). These payments, financed through loans from French banks, crippled Haiti's economy for over a century.

The country that had fought most fiercely for freedom was punished not for tyranny, but for having the audacity to live out France's democratic ideals more fully than France ever dared.

C. The Erasure of the Black Revolution

To this day, the Haitian Revolution remains marginalized in the mainstream telling of Western democratic development. It is rarely mentioned alongside the American or French Revolutions, despite its global impact. Why?

Because it challenged not only colonialism, but **the racial foundation of the Enlightenment**.

In their defiance, Haitian revolutionaries revealed a truth the West was not prepared to face: that Black people could lead, organize, and govern without permission, and that liberty, once claimed, would not wait to be granted.

The Haitian Revolution also exposed the hypocrisy of Western democracy's gatekeepers. When people of color exercised power, demanded autonomy, and reimagined the social contract outside of Europe, they were not hailed as liberators; they were treated as threats.

"The Black revolutionaries in Haiti," writes CLR James, "did not wait to be emancipated. They seized their freedom, and in doing so, terrified the Western world" (*The Black Jacobins*, 315).

D. French "Democracy" and Its Colonial Core

Beyond Haiti, the French Revolution had little interest in extending liberty to its other colonies. Algeria remained under military rule. Indochina was soon exploited for labor and resources. French West Africa became a laboratory for racialized control under the banner of "assimilation." Democracy became **domestic**, while the empire remained global.

Even the concept of "citizenship" was racialized. The 19th-century French state offered assimilation, the right to become French, but only to those who abandoned their languages, religions, and customs. You could become "equal," but only by becoming **someone else**.

This dual logic, democracy at home, domination abroad, would resonate through later empires, including those of the British, Americans, and others. It was a blueprint for managing contradiction, the ability to speak of equality while denying it in practice.

Conclusion: A Guillotine for Kings, a Muzzle for Colonies

The French Revolution inspired dreams of liberation around the world, but it also exposed the limits of Enlightenment democracy. Its failure to extend equality to the enslaved, the colonized, and the racialized marked a turning point: it became clear that Western democracy was not inherently universal. It was selective **emancipation**, wrapped in rhetoric but bound by race, empire, and profit.

The revolution that shouted *liberté* also whispered betrayal. Moreover, those who listened closely, from Haiti to Hanoi, would never forget.

Works Cited

Dubois, Laurent. *Avengers of the New World: The Story of the Haitian Revolution*. Harvard University Press, 2004.

Geggus, David. *The Haitian Revolution: A Documentary History*. Hackett Publishing, 2014.

James, C.L.R. *The Black Jacobins: Toussaint L'Ouverture and the San Domingo Revolution*. Vintage, 1989.

VII. Exporting the Myth, Democracy's Early Branding Campaign

How the West Turned Liberty into a Weapon and a Billboard

There is a difference between living an idea and **selling** it. Moreover, somewhere between the guillotines of Paris and the Constitution Hall in Philadelphia, democracy stopped being just a form of governance and became something slicker, shinier, and far more dangerous, a **brand**.

Once born in the fires of revolution, messy, imperfect, and forged by real people aching for dignity, democracy was cleaned up, repackaged, and launched as the West's most seductive export. Not a gift freely given, but a standard imposed. A moral badge worn by empires with blood on their boots.

By the 19th century, the Western world was not only practicing democracy but also *marketing* it. Not as something humble and evolving, but as a finished product. Proof of superiority. A reason to conquer.

Moreover, like any brand campaign, it came with slogans, packaging, and a lie too big to question.

A. Liberty Rebranded: The Civilizing Lie

By the late 1800s, European empires were deeply entrenched in lands they did not own, governing people they did not understand, and extracting resources they never intended to compensate for. However, conquest alone was not enough; it had to be **justified**. That is where democracy came in. Not the real kind, the kind that grows slowly and painfully from below, but the mythic kind, imported in crates stamped *civilization*, *progress*, *order*.

Thus, the colonizer dressed up as the liberator.

When Rudyard Kipling penned *The White Man's Burden* in 1899, he was not being poetic; he was handing Western powers their talking points. He urged the United States to take up the mantle of "civilizing" non-European peoples, particularly in the newly acquired Philippines. He described them, the colonized, as "half-devil and half-child." That is how the empire justified its chains: not as cruelty, but as a form of discipline.

Never mind that the people being "civilized" had complex societies, histories, and governance systems of their own. Never mind that they had languages, laws, and literatures predating anything built in Europe. The myth needed to be simple: **We bring democracy. They bring dirt.**

Thus, democracy became a cloak, a beautiful one, for domination.

B. America's Turn: From Colonies to Colonial Power

The United States was founded by men who rebelled against an empire. However, it did not take long before they became what they had despised.

By the mid-19th century, America was marching westward under the banner of *Manifest Destiny*, not just a land grab, but a holy mission. This was not an expansion, we were told. It was enlightenment. The slaughter of Native peoples, the forced removals, the assimilation schools, the broken treaties, all of it was wrapped in a story that said, *"We are giving you freedom."*

However, the graves said otherwise.

After the U.S. defeated Spain in 1898, it claimed Cuba, Puerto Rico, Guam, and the Philippines. Furthermore, in the Philippines, democracy came with bayonets. From 1899 to 1902, over 200,000 Filipinos died as U.S. forces tried to "pacify" resistance. General Jacob H. Smith ordered his men to kill anyone over the age of ten. Senator Albert Beveridge declared, from the floor of Congress, that Filipinos "must be governed by the best, and that is us."

That was democracy speaking, or rather, **democracy weaponized**, with the ballot box in one hand. The rifle is in the other.

Moreover, to this day, textbooks still claim that this was "spreading freedom." However, to the bodies buried in Balangiga and Batangas, it looked remarkably like an empire.

C. Case Study: Nigeria, A Colonial Constitution with No Soul

When the British seized control of what we now call Nigeria, they did not bring democracy, they brought a script, indirect rule. Divide and conquer. They installed empires and chiefs who answered not to the people, but to London. They drew borders that cut through ethnic nations, smashed together rival communities, and called it a country. They held "consultations," but never listened. They wrote "constitutions," but never honored them.

By the time Nigeria got its independence in 1960, it had inherited a shell, the external structure of a democracy without the internal wiring. No history of accountable governance. No tradition of participatory politics. Just the wreckage of British colonialism and a ticking time bomb of ethnic tensions left to explode.

The same story played out across the continent and the Caribbean: Ghana, Kenya, Sudan, Guyana. The forms of democracy were present, flags, anthems, parliaments, but they were all hollow, built on foundations that had never been allowed to set correctly.

This wasn't democracy delivered. It was **democracy sabotaged before birth**.

D. Missionaries, Schools, and the War on Memory

However, the colonizer's genius did not stop with guns or government. The real victory was **mental**. Once they had stolen the land, they came for the mind.

Missionaries replaced oral history with scripture. Colonial education taught Shakespeare but erased the legacy of Shaka Zulu. In Senegal, kids learned about the French Revolution, but nothing about Sundiata Keita. In India, students were taught to admire the House of Lords but not the wisdom of the Vedas. Democracy was taught not as one option among many, but as the *only* option. And not just any democracy, **Western democracy**, dressed in Enlightenment ideals, stripped of cultural context, and sold as salvation.

It was intellectual colonization. An erasure so complete that many of the colonized forgot that their ancestors once governed with grace through councils, matrilineal systems, elders' courts, rotational leadership, and communal accountability.

Moreover, many people still struggle to remember today.

"They made us hate our governance systems and then blamed us when theirs did not work here," one Kenyan scholar told me. *"That is not development. That is sabotage with a smile."*

E. Aid as a Trojan Horse

In the post-colonial era, democracy's branding got even more polished. Now it has arrived via NGOs. Via the IMF. Via "development assistance" with conditions attached. "You want aid? Privatize your water system. You want funding? Adopt our electoral model. You want legitimacy? Align your foreign policy with ours."

Democracy became a passport, and those without the proper stamp were denied access to trade, recognition, and voice. It was not democracy by consent, it was democracy by **coercion**.

Moreover, when countries pushed back, like Venezuela, Iran, and Zimbabwe, they were labeled "anti-democratic." Sanctioned. Sabotaged. Alternatively, worse, it was invaded.

Conclusion: A Roar with No Soul

The West did not just export democracy. It **branded** it. Moreover, in doing so, it flattened the complexities of self-rule into a one-size-fits-all ideology, to be adopted wholesale or risk being left behind.

What began as a political experiment became an identity. What began as a call for self-determination became a justification for global domination.

The myth of Western democracy was not just told, it was sold.

Moreover, the price was **memory**, **autonomy**, and **truth**.

Now, the world is waking up.

The question is no longer whether democracy is good,

but whether the version we have been sold is even real.

Works Cited

Beveridge, Albert. *Congressional Record*, U.S. Senate, 1900.

Falola, Toyin, and Matthew M. Heaton. *A History of Nigeria*. Cambridge University Press, 2008.

Ferguson, Niall. *Empire: The Rise and Demise of the British World Order and the Lessons for Global Power*. Basic Books, 2004.

Kramer, Paul. *The Blood of Government: Race, Empire, the United States, and the Philippines*. University of North Carolina Press, 2006.

Kipling, Rudyard. *The White Man's Burden*. 1899.

Chapter 2:

Building a Domestic Empire, How Democracy Was Used to Consolidate Internal Power

The Myth of Equality, the Machinery of Control

Introduction: A Republic Built to Rule Its Own

The myth is familiar: America, born in defiance of tyranny, stood as the world's first modern republic, a democratic beacon against empire. That is how the textbooks say it. That is the gospel repeated from classrooms to campaign stages: that the United States was different because it was *founded for the people*, by people who knew what it meant to live under oppression.

However, what if that is only half the story?

What if the real story is darker, more complicated, and more urgent?

Because while the United States preached liberty, it built something else alongside it: an **internal empire**, carefully constructed behind the curtain of the democratic process. One that corralled the Indigenous, policed the Black body, exploited the working poor, and kept political power concentrated in the hands of property-owning men, then corporations, then billionaires. All while assuring the rest of us that this was freedom.

This chapter is not about foreign policy or distant wars. It is about the battlefield within the borders of the republic, within the laws we were told were just, within a system that used the language of rights to enforce obedience.

We trace the evolution of democracy as a discipline.

How Elections Became a Ritual to Validate Inequality.

How the vote, the courts, the schools, and the streets were used to build a domestic empire that rivaled any foreign conquest.

This is not a story of ideals betrayed.

It's a story of systems designed.

Because democracy in America was not simply corrupted, it was **built with limits** baked in. Limits on who could vote, who could own land, who counted as a citizen, and who got to speak without fear.

From the founding of the republic to the rise of the carceral state, we will follow the blueprint of domestic control:

- Through the theft of Native lands,
- The enforcement of slavery under constitutional silence,
- The brutal suppression of labor and protest,
- And the slow, bureaucratic violence of poverty, surveillance, and redlined dreams.

We will meet the voices who warned us. Frederick Douglass, Ida B. Wells, Vine Deloria Jr., Bayard Rustin, Angela Davis. We will revisit the uprisings they witnessed, the truths they lived, and the price they paid for telling them.

Moreover, we will ask:

If democracy in America has always required some to be silenced, stolen from, or erased, then whose democracy is this?

The lion of Western democracy roared of liberty. However, here at home, it was also built. Moreover, in this chapter, we examine just how tightly that roar was wound around the levers of control.

II. Settler Democracy and the Displacement of Indigenous Nations

A Republic Built on Removal

Before the first ballot was cast, before the first president was sworn in, and before democracy was etched into stone in Philadelphia, the American project had already made one thing clear. This **land would belong to some, and not to others**.

The founding fathers spoke often of freedom, but they measured it in acres. Democracy, to them, was inseparable from ownership, especially ownership of land that had first to be seized, cleared, renamed, and remade. That land was Indigenous. That freedom was someone else's captivity.

The birth of American democracy was soaked in **displacement**. Its expansion came not through consent but through conquest. Moreover, as settlers moved westward with muskets and Bibles, democracy moved with them, **not as liberation**, but as **justification**.

The Doctrine of Discovery: Legalizing Theft

The United States inherited a sinister piece of colonial logic from Europe: The **Doctrine of Discovery**. First articulated by papal decree in the 15th century and later upheld by the U.S. Supreme Court in *Johnson v. M'Intosh* (1823), it stated that European powers could claim any land not occupied by Christians.

Let that sink in. In a country that would later pride itself on religious freedom, the **foundation of land law was based on religious supremacy and colonial erasure**.

This legal framework made Indigenous nations invisible in the eyes of the law. Their sovereignty did not matter. Their systems of governance, land stewardship, and cultural memory were deemed primitive. In the American imagination, they were savages to be civilized, obstacles to be removed, or remnants to be archived.

"The land did not belong to us," wrote Vine Deloria Jr., "because to them, we were never real nations. Just shadows standing in the way of their dream" (*God Is Red*).

The Indian Removal Act of 1830: Democracy's First Ethnic Cleansing

Signed into law by President Andrew Jackson, the **Indian Removal Act** authorized the forced relocation of tens of thousands of Indigenous people from their ancestral lands in the Southeast to areas west of the Mississippi River. This was not a tragedy. It was a policy. A democratic decision, made by elected leaders, ratified by Congress, carried out by soldiers.

The most infamous chapter was the **Trail of Tears**, the brutal march of the Cherokee Nation from Georgia to what is now Oklahoma. Over 4,000 died of starvation, disease, and exposure. However, Jackson was celebrated as a populist hero, a man of the people. Nevertheless, the "people" he served were white settlers hungry for land.

Democracy did not stop this. It enabled it.

What we often fail to admit is that removal was not a betrayal of American values. It was an expression of them, **the version of democracy designed for settlers**.

The Reservation System: Internal Colonies on Native Soil

After removal came containment. Indigenous nations were herded onto reservations, deliberately chosen areas with poor soil, limited water, and no proximity to economic centers. In exchange for stolen land, they were promised rations, peace, and recognition.

Instead, they received **broken treaties**, militarized surveillance, and the criminalization of their cultural practices. Spiritual ceremonies were outlawed. Children were taken from families and forced into boarding schools where their languages were beaten out of them, and their braids were cut.

The message was clear: assimilation or extinction.

Furthermore, all the while, the myth of American democracy continued to march on. The same nation that banned the Lakota from practicing the Ghost Dance was lecturing the world about religious freedom. The same government that lied in over 370 treaties with Indigenous nations (and broke nearly everyone) called itself the land of laws.

Case Study: The Dawes Act and the Theft of Native Land

In 1887, Congress passed the **Dawes Act**, which aimed to "Americanize" Native people by dividing communal landholdings and distributing individual plots to Native families. The surplus land? Sold to white settlers.

In less than 50 years, Indigenous nations lost **over 90 million acres**, an area roughly the size of Montana.

They were told this was progress. That it would make them "civilized," teach them responsibility, and bring them into the democratic fold. However, in truth, it was economic warfare disguised as reform.

The Dawes Act was not just about land. It was about **erasing an entire worldview**, one based on communal care, stewardship, and collective memory. It tried to replace kinship with contracts and sovereignty with dependency.

Myth of Shared Democracy

To this day, Indigenous people remain political ghosts in a nation they predate by millennia. Their communities face some of the highest rates of poverty, suicide, and police violence in the country. Their land continues to be exploited for pipelines, uranium, and lithium, essential to the modern economy but deadly to their ecosystems.

However, Native resistance remains fierce. From **Standing Rock** to the fight to protect Oak Flat, from cultural revitalization to legal reclamation, Indigenous nations have refused to vanish.

They remind us that democracy is not a finished product. Moreover, it cannot call itself just while it rests on broken treaties, mass graves, and silenced languages.

Conclusion: A Democracy with Blood in the Soil

The American Republic did not simply rise on the wings of liberty; it rose on the ashes of Indigenous sovereignty. What is called expansion, others lived as removal. What is called development, others felt was genocide.

Furthermore, while the founders were writing about "unalienable rights," Native families were burying their dead along forced migration routes, wondering where exactly they fit in this new democratic order.

The lion roared in Washington, but it trampled Wounded Knee, Sand Creek, and Bear River.

Moreover, the jungle remembers.

Works Cited (Preliminary)

Deloria, Vine, Jr. *God Is Red: A Native View of Religion*. Fulcrum Publishing, 2003.

Dunbar-Ortiz, Roxanne. *An Indigenous Peoples' History of the United States*. Beacon Press, 2014.

Wilkins, David E., and Heidi Kiiwetinepinesiik Stark. *American Indian Politics and the American Political System*. Rowman & Littlefield, 2017.

Banner, Stuart. *How the Indians Lost Their Land: Law and Power on the Frontier*. Harvard University Press, 2005.

III. The Enslaved Republic, Building the South and Enriching the North

Cotton, Chains, and the Constitution

If American democracy was built on the promise of freedom, then it must also account for the truth that it was physically built, **brick by brick, rail by rail, dollar by dollar**, on the backs of enslaved people. The myth tells us that democracy was about rising against the monarchy. However, the reality is this: while Jefferson spoke of liberty in Philadelphia, he was also calculating crop yields at Monticello, kept profitable by people he owned.

This was not hypocrisy. It was designed.

The United States was founded as a **slaveholding republic**. Furthermore, slavery was not simply a Southern sin; it was a **national institution**, protected by law, funded by Northern capital, and embedded in the democratic structure itself.

The Constitution's Complicity

When the framers gathered in 1787 to draft the U.S. Constitution, slavery was the unspoken guest at the table. They did not name it, but they protected it.

The Three-Fifths Clause allowed slaveholding states to count enslaved people as three-fifths of a person for purposes of representation, inflating the political power of the very states that denied them humanity.

The Fugitive Slave Clause mandated the return of escaped enslaved people to their owners, even across state lines.

The Electoral College itself was shaped by the need to protect Southern slaveholding interests from being outvoted by more populous free states.

This was not a flaw. It was a feature, **a democratic framework built to accommodate bondage**.

As legal scholar Derrick Bell wrote, "The Constitution was never colorblind. It was stained from the beginning."

Slavery as National Infrastructure

By the early 1800s, slavery was not just a regional practice; it was the **engine of the American economy**. Cotton, grown by enslaved labor in the South, fed textile mills in New England. Northern banks financed Southern plantations. Wall Street itself began as a slave trading post in Lower Manhattan.

Enslaved people were not just laborers. They were capital. By 1860, they represented over $3 billion in value, more than all the railroads and factories in America combined (Baptist 321).

However, they had no voice. No rights. No place in the democratic process where their sweat, blood, and broken bodies are subsidized.

Case Study: Georgetown University and the Sale of 272 Enslaved Persons

In 1838, facing financial hardship, the Jesuits of Georgetown University sold 272 enslaved people from Maryland plantations to buyers in Louisiana to save the school from bankruptcy. These were fathers, mothers, children, human beings whose sale kept a revered American university afloat.

For over 175 years, the story was buried. Only recently did the university begin to acknowledge its debt, and even then, reconciliation has been slow, fraught, and incomplete.

This was not a unique scandal. It was a **national pattern**. Dozens of elite institutions, such as Harvard, Yale, Brown, and Princeton, were either built by enslaved hands or funded by profits derived from slavery.

Nevertheless, in their lecture halls and democratic theory courses, those same schools would teach the Enlightenment as if it were pure, as if liberty had not first walked through slavery's shadow.

The Silence of the Ballot

In 1860, on the eve of the Civil War, nearly 4 million people lived as property in a nation that called itself free. Not even one of them had the right to vote. They could not testify in court, have their own property, or marry legally. Their children could be sold. Their bodies could be whipped at will. Their very existence was commodified, counted, and then erased from civic life.

What does it say about democracy when it coexists with this kind of cruelty?

What does it say about the soul of a nation when it is built on contracts written in cursive while people cry in chains?

North and South: A Complicity Shared

Too often, we comfort ourselves with the story that the North was on the "right side" of history, the anti-slavery region that eventually went to war to end the moral blight. However, the truth is more complicated.

Northern merchants insured slave ships. Banks in Boston and New York offered lines of credit to plantation owners, and universities invested in companies tied to the cotton trade. Even abolitionist voices, such as Lincoln's, were hesitant in granting full Black citizenship and equality.

Slavery was America's original stimulus package, and **democracy grew strong in its shadow**.

Conclusion: The Republic's Rotten Core

Democracy in the United States was never universal. From its founding, it drew sharp lines around who counted, who mattered, and who could participate.

Moreover, while the Constitution rang with ideals, it also quietly held the keys to the whip. The enslaved were the backbone of a nation that declared all men equal, but did not mean them. They were the uncounted builders of a republic that called itself righteous.

This was not an oversight.

This was the architecture.

The lion roared about liberty, but chains fed it.

Furthermore, even now, the echo of that system lingers in prisons, in poverty, in the unspoken debt still owed.

Works Cited

Baptist, Edward E. *The Half Has Never Been Told: Slavery and the Making of American Capitalism*. Basic Books, 2014.
Bell, Derrick. *Race, Racism, and American Law*. Aspen Publishers, 2008.
Wilder, Craig Steven. *Ebony and Ivy: Race, Slavery, and the Troubled History of America's Universities*. Bloomsbury Press, 2013.
Du Bois, W.E.B. *Black Reconstruction in America, 1860–1880*. Free Press, 1998.

IV. Reconstruction, Reversal, and the Rise of Jim Crow

Democracy's Brief Window, Then the Backlash

For one fleeting moment, America tried. It tried.

After the Civil War, the United States stood on the edge of transformation. The shackles had been broken. The enslaved had been legally freed. Furthermore, for the first time in the nation's history, **Black Americans stood at the threshold of democracy**, not as shadows but as citizens.

What followed between 1865 and 1877 was the most radical experiment in multiracial democracy the country had ever seen or would ever see again. Nevertheless, just as quickly as it opened, the door was slammed shut. The backlash was not only violent but also **strategic, legal, and enduring**.

Reconstruction remains a wound in the American story because it was a promise made and a promise betrayed. A glimpse of what this nation could have been, before it chose power over progress.

Reconstruction: America's Most Democratic Moment

In the immediate aftermath of the Civil War, the U.S. Congress passed three transformative amendments:

- **The 13th Amendment** abolished slavery.
- **The 14th Amendment** guaranteed equal protection under the law.
- **The 15th Amendment** protected the right to vote, regardless of race.

These were not just legal reforms; they were a rebirth. For the first time, formerly enslaved men could vote, hold office, serve on juries, and build institutions of their own. In states like South Carolina and Mississippi, Black legislators held majorities in state assemblies. Schools were built. Freedmen's Bureaus offered food and legal aid. Churches became civic centers. Black families reunited across miles of postwar wreckage.

It was fragile, messy, and imperfect, but it was real.

As W.E.B. Du Bois wrote in *Black Reconstruction*, "The slave went free; stood a brief moment in the sun; then moved back again toward slavery."

The Reversal Begins: White Supremacy Reloaded

The backlash came swiftly, and not just from unreconstructed Confederates. It came from Northern business elites, Southern planters, and federal officials who saw racial equality as a threat to **economic and political order**.

The first wave was **terrorism**.

White supremacist groups like the Ku Klux Klan and the White League did not just burn crosses; they assassinated politicians, massacred voters, and waged psychological warfare on newly freed communities. Black families were driven from their homes. Schools were torched. Anyone daring to exercise their rights faces mutilation or murder.

Case Study: The Colfax Massacre (1873)

In Louisiana, a violent white militia overran a courthouse where Black citizens had sought protection after a contested election. Over 150 Black men were slaughtered, some execution-style, after surrendering. The federal government responded with silence. The courts responded with precedent. In *United States v. Cruikshank* (1876), the Supreme Court ruled that the federal government could not prosecute private individuals for civil rights violations, effectively **legalizing racial terrorism**.

From Reconstruction to Jim Crow: Building a Racial Caste System

Once federal troops were withdrawn from the South in 1877 as part of the Hayes-Tilden Compromise, the fragile protections of Reconstruction collapsed. The era that followed **Jim Crow** was not simply a return to segregation. It was the **codification of white supremacy**.

- **Poll taxes**, **literacy tests**, and **grandfather clauses** ensured that Black voters were disenfranchised without openly violating the 15th Amendment.
- **Convict leasing systems** re-enslaved Black men for petty crimes, funneling them into chain gangs that built railroads, picked cotton, and fed state coffers.
- **Segregation laws** divided every corner of life, from schools to train cars to drinking fountains.
- And **lynching** became a public ritual, a spectacle of racial terror, often with children in attendance and postcards sold as souvenirs.

Between 1880 and 1950, more than 4,000 documented lynchings took place in the American South. These were not just acts of violence. They were **warnings**.

Black life in Jim Crow America was life under occupation, a democracy in name, but a caste system in practice.

Case Study: Wilmington, North Carolina (1898)

In what is now acknowledged as the only successful coup d'état on U.S. soil, white supremacists in Wilmington overthrew a legally elected multiracial government, burned Black businesses, and murdered dozens of Black residents. The city's thriving Black middle class was destroyed overnight. Newspapers celebrated it. The federal government looked away. The perpetrators were never punished. **This was democracy defeated by mob rule** and made possible by silence at the top.

The North Was Not Innocent

While Jim Crow is most often associated with the South, the **North had its ways of maintaining racial hierarchy**: redlining, employment discrimination, police violence, and school segregation through zoning and funding disparities. Cities like Chicago, Boston, and New York enforced residential apartheid without ever writing it into state constitutions.

In this so-called "land of the free," race determined everything: your access to education, your right to vote, your treatment by the police, even your life expectancy.

Furthermore, the democracy that once held such promise. It was now a thin veil over institutionalized racism.

Conclusion: Democracy Undone

Reconstruction offered a glimpse of what America could become: a pluralistic, participatory, multiracial democracy. That window was slammed shut, not just by mobs and militias, but by legislatures, judges, and presidents who decided that white supremacy was easier to manage than justice.

This was not democracy's failure.

It was democracy **being recalibrated to serve the interests of power**.

Furthermore, its legacy still lingers, visible in every voter ID law, every racially gerrymandered district, every underfunded Black school, every courtroom where justice bends toward whiteness.

The wounded lion limps not because its enemies struck it from the outside, but because it **betrayed its promise from within**.

Works Cited

Alexander, Michelle. *The New Jim Crow: Mass Incarceration in the Age of Colorblindness*. New Press, 2010.

Blackmon, Douglas A. *Slavery by Another Name: The Re-Enslavement of Black Americans from the Civil War to World War II*. Anchor Books, 2008.

Du Bois, W.E.B. *Black Reconstruction in America, 1860–1880*. Free Press, 1998.

Equal Justice Initiative. *Lynching in America: Confronting the Legacy of Racial Terror*. EJI, 2017.

Gilmore, Glenda Elizabeth. *Gender and Jim Crow: Women and the Politics of White Supremacy in North Carolina, 1896–1920*. University of North Carolina Press, 1996.

V. The Industrial State, Capitalism, Class, and Controlled Labor

Democracy for the Few, Discipline for the Many

As the 19th century gave way to the 20th, America grew taller, its cities filled with smoke and steel, its railroads stitched the continent, and its factories buzzed with the sound of modernity. The Industrial Revolution had arrived, and with it came staggering wealth, breathtaking innovation, and a new form of quiet violence.

This era is often romanticized as the "age of invention," a triumph of democracy married to free enterprise. Nevertheless, look closer, and the gleam of industry gives way to the grime of exploitation. For every tycoon who climbed the ladder, millions held **the ladder steadily and never saw the top**.

This was not democracy expanding. It was being **hollowed out**, repurposed to serve capital, while poverty, police, and policy silenced those who built the machines of wealth.

The Gilded Age: When Democracy Served the Market

The late 1800s saw the birth of America's billionaire class. Rockefeller. Carnegie. Morgan. Vanderbilt. Their names still adorn libraries, universities, and foundations, but their empires were forged in sweatshops, coal mines, and blood-soaked strikes.

Elections still occurred. Congress still met. However, power, **real power,** had shifted. It was no longer rooted in the ballot box. It was tied to the vault.

In 1895, banker J.P. Morgan bailed out the U.S. Treasury with a private loan, essentially renting the nation its currency. That was not capitalism regulated by democracy. That was democracy **mortgaged to capital**.

The Supreme Court gave corporations the legal status of people in *Santa Clara County v. Southern Pacific Railroad* (1886). However, the actual people, immigrants, women, and children working in textile mills and steel plants had no authentic voice. The vote meant little if the factory owned your time, your body, and your neighborhood.

Case Study: The Pullman Strike (1894)

After the Pullman Company cut wages but refused to lower rent in its company-owned housing, thousands of railway workers walked off the job. Their strike, coordinated by the American Railway Union under Eugene V. Debs, paralyzed freight traffic and disrupted mail service.

President Grover Cleveland responded not with negotiation, but with the **U.S. Army**. Soldiers opened fire on the strikers. Debs were arrested. The federal government had sided not with workers, but with the very company that caused the crisis.

Democracy did not die that day. It simply showed us who it served.

Immigrant Labor and the Machinery of Exploitation

The industrial boom needed bodies. Thus, it turned to immigrants, Irish, Italian, Chinese, Jewish, Polish, and later, Mexican. They arrived at Ellis Island and Angel Island with hope, only to find **factories that reduced them to ashes**.

- Twelve-hour shifts.
- No safety regulations.
- No child labor laws.
- Tenements where disease spread faster than wages.
- And bosses who spoke of freedom but demanded obedience.

The Chinese Exclusion Act of 1882 became the first significant federal immigration restriction, targeting a group whose labor built the railroads but whose presence was deemed a "threat" to white American democracy.

Labor built this country, but labor, predominantly **non-white, non-English speaking labor**- was treated as disposable.

The War on Labor Unions: Criminalizing Collective Power

As workers organized, the state responded with increased repression. Unions were painted as anarchist, foreign, and communist. Labor leaders were jailed, blacklisted, or killed. The government became the enforcer for big business, weaponizing courts and police against organizing efforts.

The First Red Scare (1919–1920) was not about protecting democracy; it was about protecting profit. Strikes were framed as sedition. Immigrants were deported without trial. Entire movements for fair wages and dignity were labeled "un-American."

Democracy was not a shared table. It was a gated estate with labor outside the walls.

Gendered Exploitation: Women as Invisible Engines

Women powered entire sectors of the industrial economy, including textile factories, domestic labor, and garment workshops. However, they were paid less, harassed more, and denied access to political voices until the 20th century. Their work was essential but **erased**. Their organizing efforts, such as the Bread and Roses Strike in 1912, revealed both their economic strength and the brutal repression they faced.

Even within progressive movements, women were often told to wait their turn. Democracy had a gender, and it was not female.

The American Dream, Bought and Sold

By the 1920s, the mythology of the "American Dream" was fully formed: work hard, play by the rules, and you will succeed. Nevertheless, for millions of workers, mainly immigrants, Black Southerners who migrated north, and those living in company towns, this dream was a lie. The rules were **rigged**, and the system had no intention of changing.

What passed for democracy was often just consent manufacturing, voting for candidates financed by the same tycoons who cut your pay. Furthermore, even when workers tried to use the democratic system, organizing, striking, testifying, they met not with laws, but with **batons**.

Conclusion: Labor Without Voice, Industry Without Justice

The industrial state taught America how to praise democracy while crushing its spirit. It taught generations to believe in freedom while living in fear of hunger, pink slips, and police raids. It expanded the economy while contracting the soul.

Here, democracy served as a shield, not for the people, but for the market.
Furthermore, capitalism, unchecked by conscience, devoured the very

workers who built its golden towers.

The domestic empire was not merely a political entity. It was economic.
Furthermore, the lion of liberty was fed by those it never let speak.

Works Cited

Debs, Eugene V. *Walls and Bars*. Charles H. Kerr Publishing, 1927.

Fink, Leon. *Labor's Search for Political Order: The Political Behavior of the American Working Class*. University of Illinois Press, 1992.

Klein, Naomi. *The Shock Doctrine: The Rise of Disaster Capitalism*. Picador, 2007.

Zinn, Howard. *A People's History of the United States*. Harper Perennial, 2005.

Woloch, Nancy. *Women and the American Experience: A Concise History*. McGraw-Hill, 2001.

VI. The Rise of the Surveillance State

From the Sedition Act to the Patriot Act

For a nation that claims to prize freedom above all else, America has devoted an extraordinary amount of time, money, and effort to monitoring **its people**.

It began with fear. It always begins with fear.

First, there was fear of sedition. Then communism. Then radicals. Then Muslims. Then the protesters. Throughout history, the state told its citizens: You are either with us or against us. Moreover, those who dared to dissent, ask tough questions, resist unjust wars, organize strikes, or defend civil rights were scrutinized. Or worse.

This was not national security.
This was **domestic empire maintenance**.
It was not about protecting democracy from enemies abroad.

It was about protecting power from the people within.

The Sedition Acts: Criminalizing Dissent

In 1798, just over ten years after the Constitution was ratified, President John Adams signed the Alien and Sedition Acts, which made criticizing the federal government a crime. Newspapers were shut down, immigrants were deported, and political opponents were jailed. The First Amendment's protections had barely been established.

A century later, pressured by World War I, President Woodrow Wilson revived the idea. The Espionage Act of 1917 and the Sedition Act of 1918 made it illegal to criticize the government, the military, or even the flag.

Socialist Eugene Debs was sentenced to 10 years in prison for giving a speech opposing the draft. His crime? Quoting the Constitution too boldly for the state's comfort.

This was not the fringe. These were federal laws, signed by presidents and enforced by judges, that **made patriotism compulsory and protest a crime**.

Surveillance and the Birth of the FBI

The 20th century saw the formal institutionalization of surveillance. The **Federal Bureau of Investigation**, established to address interstate crime, quickly evolved into a tool for **political policing**.

Under J. Edgar Hoover, the FBI compiled millions of files on U.S. citizens, journalists, clergy, professors, union leaders, and civil rights activists. Their phone calls were tapped. Their mail was intercepted. Their personal lives were smeared in the press. Their deaths were sometimes **engineered and covered up**.

Case Study: COINTELPRO, Dismantling Democracy from Within

From 1956 to 1971, the FBI operated **COINTELPRO** (Counter-Intelligence Program), targeting civil rights organizations, Black liberation groups, anti-war activists, and Native resistance leaders.

- Martin Luther King Jr. was surveilled, harassed, and blackmailed.
- Fred Hampton of the Black Panther Party was assassinated in his sleep by the Chicago police working with the FBI.
- American Indian Movement leaders were infiltrated, discredited, and jailed on trumped-up charges.
- The anti-Vietnam War movement was portrayed as a domestic threat worthy of infiltration and subversion.

COINTELPRO did not protect democracy. It **undermined it**, from within the very agencies meant to uphold it.

It showed that the state would rather crush the protest than confront the truths the protest revealed.

Immigrant Communities and the Language of Loyalty

Surveillance in America has always had a racial and ethnic target. In the early 20th century, it was anarchist Italian immigrants who were involved. In the mid-century, it was Japanese Americans, **120,000 of whom were rounded up and imprisoned during World War II without a single charge of espionage ever proven**.

In the post-9/11 era, surveillance turned its gaze toward **Muslim, Arab, and South Asian Americans**. Entire mosques were infiltrated. Community centers were monitored. Children's online activity was flagged. Airports became racial sorting grounds. The state told them, 'Prove your loyalty.' Daily. Alternatively, live under suspicion forever.

This wasn't about a few bad policies. It was about a system **trained to fear the margins**.

The Patriot Act: Democracy in the Rearview

After the September 11th attacks, Congress passed the **USA PATRIOT Act**. This sweeping surveillance law gave the federal government unprecedented access to citizens' emails, phone records, bank accounts, and private lives.

Passed with almost no public debate and signed into law by President George W. Bush, the act signaled a turning point: **fear had become law**.

- Geofence warrants allow police to sweep up the digital data of everyone near a protest or crime scene.
- Stingray devices mimic cell towers, tricking phones into giving up their location.
- Facial recognition software is quietly deployed at airports, protests, and on public transit, often with racial bias embedded in its design.

The state now collects data **not because you are guilty**, but because you exist.

Furthermore, if democracy is supposed to mean privacy, autonomy, and voice, then this is not democracy.

Case Study: Black Lives Matter and the Digital Dragnet

During the 2020 BLM uprisings, federal and local agencies deployed aerial drones, facial recognition software, and cellphone tracking to monitor protesters in real-time. Social media accounts were flagged. Activists were doxed. Police used burner accounts to infiltrate organizing chats.

The same tactics used in counterterrorism abroad were now being applied to citizens exercising their First Amendment rights.

If protest is a democratic expression, then surveillance is the modern **muzzle**, silent, invisible, and all-seeing.

Conclusion: The Gaze That Never Sleeps

The American state has learned to **look** rather than **listen**. To survey rather than serve. To punish speech rather than heed it. It fears unrest more than injustice, and so it watches. Always.

Nevertheless, surveillance does not make democracy stronger. It makes it quieter.

Moreover, the quieter we become, the further we drift from anything that resembles freedom.

The lion may still roar in the halls of power, but it does so while watching its citizens from behind a two-way mirror, terrified that the people might remember the power they were promised.

Works Cited

Churchill, Ward, and Jim Vander Wall. *Agents of Repression: The FBI's Secret Wars Against the Black Panther Party and the American Indian Movement*. South End Press, 1990.

Greenwald, Glenn. *No Place to Hide: Edward Snowden, the NSA, and the U.S. Surveillance State*. Metropolitan Books, 2014.

The Intercept. "The FBI's Secret Rules." Accessed 2023.

Beydoun, Khaled A. *American Islamophobia: Understanding the Roots and Rise of Fear*. University of California Press, 2018.

ACLU. "What You Should Know About Geofence Warrants." *American Civil Liberties Union*, 2022.

Freedom of the Press Foundation. "How Police Are Surveilling Protests." 2020.

VII. The New Deal and the Price of Inclusion

Progress with Exceptions

We are often told that the New Deal saved American democracy. It was the lifeboat that pulled a drowning nation from the Great Depression. It restored faith in the state, expanded the safety net, and proved that government could be a force for good.

Nevertheless, behind every "American success story," there is always a shadow.

Yes, the New Deal transformed lives, putting people back to work, electrifying rural communities, building roads, bridges, parks, and public art. However, its benefits were **never equally shared**. It pulled some Americans into the middle class, and locked others out.

Because inclusion, in Roosevelt's America, had a price. Furthermore, that price was **racial silence**, **gendered assumptions**, and **economic obedience**.

The Deal That Was Not for Everyone

Franklin Delano Roosevelt's administration passed sweeping legislation between 1933 and 1939. The Social Security Act. The Wagner Act. The Fair Labor Standards Act. These laws built the scaffolding for modern American life. However, behind their idealism lay compromises with power brokers, especially Southern Democrats, whose support was crucial to passing any legislation.

To secure their votes, the New Deal was **designed to exclude** the people most in need:

- **Domestic workers** (mostly Black women)
- **Agricultural laborers** (predominantly Black and Mexican workers)
- **Undocumented migrants**
- **And anyone living in segregated or red-lined neighborhoods**

The Social Security Act of 1935, which guaranteed old-age pensions and unemployment insurance, specifically excluded agricultural and domestic labor, affecting **over 65% of Black workers in the South** (Katznelson 21).

These exclusions were not oversights. They were intentional. They were the price of unity with white supremacists in Congress. Thus, democracy grew, but only within the fences of whiteness and class.

Case Study: Redlining and the Creation of the White Suburb

The Federal Housing Administration (FHA), established during the New Deal, revolutionized homeownership by backing low-interest loans and stabilizing the banking system. Nevertheless, the maps it used, drawn by the Homeowners' Loan Corporation, **rated neighborhoods by racial and ethnic "risk"**.

Black neighborhoods, or those with even a single Black family, were shaded red and labeled "hazardous." Banks would not lend there. Property values plummeted. The investment fled.

Meanwhile, white families in newly developed suburbs, often with racially restrictive covenants baked into their deeds, received federal subsidies, loans, and tax advantages.

By 1960, 98% of federally backed home loans went to white borrowers (Rothstein 78).
Black Americans were told: *The American Dream is not for you.*

The long-term effects were devastating. Redlining created the wealth gap, educational segregation, environmental injustice, and the urban disinvestment that still haunts Black and brown communities today.

Labor Rights, But Not for All

The Wagner Act of 1935 gave workers the right to unionize and bargain collectively, a monumental gain for labor. However, it excluded domestic and farm workers, left out millions of immigrants, and failed to protect workers of color from being **excluded by white-only unions**.

Even when workers of color organized their unions, such as the Brotherhood of Sleeping Car Porters or the United Farm Workers, they had to fight not just against bosses, but also against the very labor movement that claimed to speak for all.

Democracy, even in the workplace, came with **color lines**.

The Myth of Government Neutrality

The New Deal painted the federal government as an impartial referee between capital and labor. However, it **protected corporate interests**, subsidized racial hierarchy, and **disciplined political dissent**.

- When Black veterans protested for equal jobs, they were labeled "troublemakers."
- When women demanded childcare support, they were told to return to domestic life.
- When radicals in the labor movement grew too bold, the FBI infiltrated their unions.

The state's generosity was always conditional, tied to obedience, loyalty, and silence.

You could receive aid, yes, nevertheless, only if you stayed in your place.

The "American Middle Class" and Manufactured Inclusion

What the New Deal built, more than anything, was the myth of a unified middle class, a buffer between the poor and the elite, crafted to absorb discontent and channel ambition into consumption.

White workers could now buy homes, cars, and appliances. Their children could attend college on the GI Bill. Their wealth grew across generations.

Meanwhile, Black, Latino, Asian, and Indigenous families were denied access to capital, boxed into underfunded neighborhoods, and criminalized when they protested.

This was not democracy expanding. It was **democracy being color-coded**.

Narrative Interlude: A House, A Loan, A Dream Denied

Imagine a Black couple in 1940s Detroit, both working, saving, trying to buy a home. They apply for a loan. The bank manager smiles, then shakes his head. *"Not in that neighborhood,"* he says. Their file is marked "high risk." The home goes to someone else.

That someone else gets a 30-year FHA-backed mortgage, a tax break, and a growing asset.

The Black couple gets rent receipts and silence.

That gap widens.

And widens.

Furthermore, by the time their children grow up, the gap is a canyon.

This was not a fluke.

It was **policy**.

Conclusion: The Deal That Made America, And Marked It

The New Deal saved American capitalism. It restored faith in the state. It proved that massive public investment could lift a nation from despair.

However, it also revealed who democracy was truly **meant to include**.

Progress came with exclusions. Equity came with conditions. Moreover, justice came at a price that millions could not afford to pay.

The lion roared again, this time with hope in its voice. However, the echoes did not reach every corner of the jungle.

Some were left behind on purpose.

Works Cited

Katznelson, Ira. *When Affirmative Action Was White: An Untold History of Racial Inequality in Twentieth Century America*. W.W. Norton & Company, 2005.

Rothstein, Richard. *The Color of Law: A Forgotten History of How Our Government Segregated America*. Liveright, 2017.

Sugrue, Thomas J. *The Origins of the Urban Crisis: Race and Inequality in Postwar Detroit*. Princeton University Press, 1996.

Jackson, Kenneth T. *Crabgrass Frontier: The Suburbanization of the United States*. Oxford University Press, 1985.

VIII. Carceral Democracy, The Empire of Prisons

From Chains to Cells

What happens when a nation abolishes slavery but never dismantles its logic?

It builds prisons.

Moreover, it calls them justice.

From the ashes of the plantation system rose a new empire, not cotton, but cages. Not of overseers, but of wardens and police. A system that did not need whips to break people, because now it has courts. Now it had the law. Now it had the illusion of due process, and a new vocabulary to carry forward the old work: **"order," "crime," "safety," "corrections."**

This was not a deviation from American democracy.

It was its **continuation**, in uniform, on paper, and behind bars.

The 13th Amendment's Loophole

When the 13th Amendment abolished slavery in 1865, it came with a poison clause:

"Neither slavery nor involuntary servitude, *except as a punishment for crime*, shall exist within the United States..."

Those five words, *except as a punishment for crime*, opened a trapdoor through which the entire apparatus of racial control could be lowered, brick by brick, into the foundations of the new American state.

Freedom was now conditional.

Black life could be re-enslaved, legally, with the stroke of a judge's pen.

Convict Leasing and Jim Crow Justice

In the decades after emancipation, Southern states passed **Black Codes**, laws that criminalized everyday behavior for newly freed people.

Loitering. Vagrancy. Speaking out of turn. Unpaid debt.

All became punishable offenses. Not because they threatened public safety, but because they offered legal means to **recapture Black labor**.

Once convicted, prisoners were leased to railroads, coal mines, and private plantations. They were starved, beaten, and worked to death. No trials. No appeal. Just forced labor rebranded.

By the 1890s, **convict leasing generated more state revenue in Alabama than all other sources combined** (Blackmon).

And democracy? It stood silent in the courtroom, holding the door open to the cellblock.

The Birth of Mass Incarceration

Fast forward a century. By the 1970s, the civil rights movement had compelled America to examine itself in the mirror, and the reflection was one of anger, defiance, and determination. Voting rights. Integration. Affirmative action.

Nevertheless, with that resistance came **a counteroffensive**, not in the streets, but in the courts and legislatures.

- **Nixon's "law and order" platform** began the war on drugs, long before the crack epidemic.

- **Reagan's escalation** turned poverty into a crime scene.
- **Clinton's 1994 Crime Bill**, co-authored by then-Senator Joe Biden, funneled billions into police departments, expanded mandatory minimums, and incentivized states to build more prisons.

By 2000, the United States had more people behind bars than any other nation on Earth, a quarter of the world's prison population.

Moreover, the numbers were not random. They were **racially engineered**.

Case Study: The Rockefeller Drug Laws and the Criminalization of Blackness

Passed in New York in 1973, the Rockefeller Drug Laws imposed mandatory minimum sentences of 15 years to life for possession of small amounts of narcotics, often less than what could fit in a pocket.

The result? A flood of young Black and brown men into the prison system, many first-time offenders, many still in their teens.

They were not treated as addicts or patients. They were labeled "super predators." Furthermore, once inside the system, they lost the right to vote, to serve on juries, to receive public housing, and to access student loans.

A single conviction became a life sentence, not of time, but of exile.

Prison Labor: Slavery's Quiet Heir

Even today, incarcerated individuals work for pennies per hour, sometimes for multinational corporations. They fight wildfires, make furniture, sew military uniforms, and clean state buildings.

They are told this is rehabilitation. However, it appears to be a form of exploitation.

In some states, refusing to work can lead to solitary confinement. That is not democracy. That is coercion with a badge.

Prison labor is not about skills. It is about **profit and punishment**, and the American economy has quietly depended on it for decades.

The Geography of Incarceration

Mass incarceration does not just punish individuals. It guts entire communities.

In neighborhoods like West Baltimore, South Side Chicago, and East Oakland, **a third of Black men have spent time behind bars**. Children grow up with parents in prison. Schools lose funding. Police became militarized. Jobs disappear. Furthermore, trauma becomes generational.

Meanwhile, rural white counties **build prisons as economic lifelines**, replacing manufacturing jobs with correctional officers and surveillance tech.

We have built a country where incarceration is not just a policy. It is **infrastructure**.

Democracy's Dead End

The most grotesque irony? People in prison are counted in the U.S. Census, boosting population numbers in the (often white) districts where they are incarcerated, but they **cannot vote**.

This is a modern-day **three-fifths compromise**: bodies used for representation without representation. A democracy that grows from the ground up, on cinderblocks and razor wire.

Conclusion: The Cage as Constitution

What is democracy if it thrives alongside mass incarceration? What is freedom if it makes room for one in every three Black boys born today to expect prison in their lifetime?

The carceral state did not emerge despite the existence of democracy. It emerged **through it**, with the help of legislators, judges, and voters who were told that punishment equals safety, and that security requires a cage.

The lion still roars. Nevertheless, now it does so behind bars, in courtrooms that wear the mask of fairness, in patrol cars that circle schools like predators.

This is the final frontier of the domestic empire: **where democracy ends, and surveillance, suspicion, and steel begin.**

Works Cited

Alexander, Michelle. *The New Jim Crow: Mass Incarceration in the Age of Colorblindness*. New Press, 2010.

Blackmon, Douglas A. *Slavery by Another Name: The Re-Enslavement of Black Americans from the Civil War to World War II*. Anchor Books, 2008.

Forman Jr., James. *Locking Up Our Own: Crime and Punishment in Black America*. Farrar, Straus and Giroux, 2017.

Davis, Angela Y. *Are Prisons Obsolete?* Seven Stories Press, 2003.

Gilmore, Ruth Wilson. *Golden Gulag: Prisons, Surplus, Crisis, and Opposition in Globalizing California*. University of California Press, 2007.

Chapter 2 Recap: Building a Domestic Empire, How Democracy Was Used to Consolidate Internal Power

For generations, the United States has sold itself as the shining city on a hill, a democracy built on freedom, fairness, and the will of the people. Nevertheless, as this chapter makes painfully clear, democracy was **always built with a double standard**. It promised liberty with one hand while consolidating control with the other.

This chapter turns inward, not to ask whether America lived up to its democratic ideals, but to **question the very blueprint itself**.

We begin with the **displacement of Indigenous peoples**, showing how settler democracy was founded on stolen land, broken treaties, and forced assimilation. From the Trail of Tears to boarding schools, the very birth of American democracy required the erasure of the First Nations who lived here.

We then confront the **enslavement of African peoples**, not as a moral failing but as a foundational structure. Enslaved labor built the wealth of the South, the infrastructure of the North, and the democratic institutions that excluded Black life by design. The Constitution protected slavery in silence, while the nation profited in full voice.

Next, we explore **Reconstruction**, the brief, brilliant window when America attempted to establish a multiracial democracy. Black voters held offices, built schools, and shaped the law. However, that window was violently slammed shut by white terror, federal retreat, and a new era of Jim Crow, where democracy was twisted into a tool of racial control.

As the nation industrialized, democracy became further **subservient to capital**. Workers toiled in brutal conditions while a new class of robber barons bought influence and manipulated elections. Immigrants, women, and children became the cheap engines of growth, but were excluded from the very system they fueled. Labor uprisings were crushed, unions infiltrated, and dissent criminalized.

With resistance rising, the state turned inward, launching **a surveillance machine** under the guise of national security. From the FBI's COINTELPRO to the Patriot Act, dissenting voices, especially those of color, were tracked, harassed, and neutralized. Freedom of speech was tolerated only when it did not threaten power.

Even the much-celebrated **New Deal** was not a democratic triumph for all. It built the modern welfare state and expanded the middle class, but only for white Americans. Black and brown workers were left out, redlined, and denied the benefits of federally backed mortgages, labor protections, and public investment.

We confront the **rise of the carceral state**, the most evident proof that American democracy has long equated control with justice. From the loophole in the 13th Amendment to mass incarceration today, the state has built an empire of cages that disproportionately targets Black, brown, and poor communities. The criminal justice system became the new plantation, cloaked in law and order.

The Core Truth of Chapter 2:

Democracy in America did not fail because of individual bad actors or a few policy missteps.

It failed, and continued to fail, because **it was never meant to serve everyone equally**.

What we call democracy at home is, in many ways, an **internal empire**, built to manage labor, contain dissent, and maintain racial and economic hierarchy beneath the illusion of freedom.

The ballot box exists.

The Constitution is quoted.

The machinery of exclusion hums beneath it all, well-oiled, well-funded, and deeply American.

The lion roared about liberty. However, here at home, it has also built walls. And cages.

Moreover, far too often, it used the language of democracy not to empower, but to **discipline**.

Chapter 3:

Exporting the Dream, The Global Selling of Democracy

Freedom for Sale, Empire in Disguise

Chapter Theme

This chapter confronts one of the most enduring myths in modern geopolitics: that the United States promotes democracy globally out of moral obligation, to uplift the oppressed, defend the weak, and guide the world toward a brighter, freer future.

However, history tells a different story.

The democracy that America exports is not the messy, participatory, justice-seeking dream born in rebellion. It is a sleek, weaponized product, mass-produced, branded in red, white, and blue, and shipped overseas with strings attached. A Trojan horse that promises ballots and delivers bases. That sells freedom but instills fear. That uses the language of liberty to cover the mechanics of empire.

This chapter exposes how democracy became America's **most seductive export**, not as a shared ideal, but as a **strategic instrument of dominance**, to open markets, dismantle sovereignty, and keep nations tethered to U.S. interests.

Whether through economic coercion, cultural colonization, military occupation, or soft power propaganda, American foreign policy wrapped its ambitions in democratic packaging, and too often, **people paid the price in blood, silence, and betrayal**.

We ask: What happens when democracy stops being a shared struggle and becomes a **product for sale**? What happens when freedom is granted conditionally, only to those who buy into the right ideology, the right policies, the right alliances?

The answer lies in the stories we will tell, of coups hidden behind constitutions, of ballots cast under surveillance, of foreign aid that comes with a leash, and of people who resisted the dream, not because they hated freedom, but because they **refused to be colonized by its mask**.

This chapter is not an indictment of democracy itself. It is a reckoning with how **its name has been hijacked**, globalized, and wielded as a cudgel by the very power that once claimed to resist the empire.

Here, we will follow the dream, from the villages of Guatemala to the oil fields of Iran, from the ballot boxes of Haiti to the bombed cities of the Middle East, and watch how it was bent into **a blueprint for obedience**.

Because when democracy becomes a weapon, liberation becomes occupation.

I. The Gospel According to Washington

How a Superpower Became a Self-Appointed Prophet of Freedom

In the aftermath of World War II, the world stood in ruins, physically, politically, and morally. Europe's cities were gutted. Colonies were on fire. Fascism had collapsed in blood, and communism had risen in its wake. In this shattered global landscape, the United States emerged not just with its economy intact, but with a **newfound identity**: the reluctant giant, the benevolent victor, the custodian of liberty.

Washington did not just build roads, fund schools, or patrol borders. It preached. Furthermore, its sermon was simple: **Democracy is salvation, and America is its missionary.**

This narrative, born of battlefield triumph and Cold War fear, would go on to shape the next seven decades of foreign policy. Furthermore, like all effective gospels, it had verses, rituals, and unquestioned truths.

The United States was not merely defending its interests. It was "defending freedom." It was not merely toppling governments. It was "liberating people."

It was not building an empire. It was "spreading democracy."

This gospel gave the American public something to believe in, and the U.S. government something to **hide behind**.

The Rhetoric of Righteousness

It began with President Truman's 1947 address to Congress, a moment that would become the blueprint for generations of global engagement.

"I believe that it must be the policy of the United States," Truman declared, "to support free peoples who are resisting attempted subjugation by armed minorities or by outside pressures."

What sounded like a moral imperative was, in truth, **a strategic doctrine**, one that greenlit American intervention anywhere socialism or anti-colonialism dared to rise. Over time, this would extend from Greece and Turkey to Vietnam, Chile, Congo, and beyond.

The "free peoples" Truman vowed to defend? Often dictators in sharp suits.
The "outside pressures" he warned of? Often, democratically elected leaders refused to play by Washington's rules.

It was a rebranding of empire, **with God, liberty, and the ballot box replacing bayonets and crowns**.

A Tale of Two Freedoms

What emerged was a **bifurcated worldview**:

1. **If you aligned with U.S. interests**, you were part of the "Free World", no matter how brutal your regime.
2. **If you challenged U.S. interests**, you were labeled a threat to democracy, even if your people elected you in fair elections.

The United States thus became both judge and jury on who qualified as "democratic." Sovereignty was respected only when it aligned with Washington's bottom line.

As historian Greg Grandin noted, "The United States did not support democracy; it supported **those who supported its version** of democracy" (*Empire's Workshop* 22).

The American dream, now turned outward, was offered to the world with conditions. You could have self-determination, but only if it were **made in America**.

The Packaging of Power

By the 1950s, the U.S. was investing heavily not only in military alliances but also in **cultural hegemony**. Hollywood exported freedom in Technicolor. The Voice of America broadcast democracy across oceans. U.S.-funded universities opened branches across the Global South. Peace Corps volunteers taught American civics in classrooms barely free of colonial chalk.

This wasn't just geopolitics. It was **global branding**, an ideological marketing campaign that told the world: *Democracy looks like us. Liberty sounds like English. And freedom wears a suit and shakes hands with a senator.*

Beneath the packaging was an open secret: this dream was selective, strategic, and often enforced at gunpoint.

The Great American Contradiction

Back home, the U.S. was still segregated, surveilling activists, and suppressing labor uprisings. Abroad, it stood tall as the world's freedom fighter.

The contradiction became unbearable.

How could a nation that lynched Black men on Sunday claim to save brown men in Southeast Asia on Monday?

People across Africa, Latin America, the Middle East, and Asia saw the contradiction. However, to many Americans, it remained invisible, obscured by speeches, slogans, and the intoxicating belief in national exceptionalism.

Conclusion: The Birth of a Doctrine, the Death of Honest Democracy

What Truman began as a Cold War strategy would evolve into a gospel, repeated by every president, Democrat or Republican, liberal or hawk. Kennedy promised to "pay any price" for liberty. Reagan called America "a shining city on a hill." Bush spoke of bringing democracy "to the darkest corners of the Earth."

However, they all spoke from the same pulpit.

Moreover, they all told the same story.

That democracy, this fragile, flawed, hard-fought human experiment, could be packaged, sold, dropped from planes, installed in parliaments, and used to justify war.

The lion roared again. However, now it roared with sanctimony. With scriptwriters. With flags satellites and aid conditions written in fine print.

And so began the age of **democracy as disguise**.

Works Cited

Grandin, Greg. *Empire's Workshop: Latin America, the United States, and the Rise of the New Imperialism*. Metropolitan Books, 2006.
Westad, Odd Arne. *The Global Cold War*. Cambridge University Press, 2005.
Hunt, Michael H. *Ideology and U.S. Foreign Policy*. Yale University Press, 2009.
Kinzer, Stephen. *Overthrow: America's Century of Regime Change from Hawaii to Iraq*. Henry Holt, 2006.

II. The Marshall Plan and the Myth of Benevolence

"Rebuilding Europe, Reshaping the World"

In American memory, the Marshall Plan is sacred. A shining example of enlightened statecraft. A generous outpouring of economic aid that helped rebuild war-ravaged Europe, cementing the U.S. as the benevolent guardian of the post-war world.

Even today, its name carries weight, invoked whenever America wants to project global leadership. A "Marshall Plan for Africa." A "Marshall Plan for climate change." A "Marshall Plan for democracy."

Nevertheless, behind the headlines and history books lies a far more complex and calculated truth: the Marshall Plan was not just a gift, it was **a bargain**. It was not just about recovery; it was about **realignment**. Moreover, while it did lift economies, it also secured markets, suppressed alternatives, and drew an iron curtain of capitalism across the continent.

This was not charity.

It was **geopolitical engineering**, packaged as kindness.

A Plan Born in Panic

When Secretary of State George C. Marshall announced the plan at Harvard in 1947, Europe was on the brink. Cities were bombed out, infrastructure destroyed, and people were starving. However, there was another fear haunting the U.S., not just poverty, but also the possibility of political upheaval.

Socialist and communist parties were gaining popularity across Western Europe. Labor strikes erupted in France. The Italian left was organizing with strength. Washington worried that desperation might lead to revolution, not unlike what had happened in Russia three decades earlier.

The Marshall Plan, then, was less about rebuilding and more about **redirecting** loyalty, ideology, and economies toward Washington's image of democracy, meaning private markets, free trade, and U.S.

influence.

"The danger to the free world," wrote one 1947 State Department memo, "is not necessarily military invasion. It is the internal collapse of friendly governments." (Westad 132)

Aid would be offered. However, there would be strings, **conditions** cloaked in assistance.

Strings Attached: The Fine Print of Freedom

To qualify for Marshall Plan funds, European nations had to **open their markets to American goods**, accept U.S.-approved economic policies, and suppress left-wing political movements seen as hostile to capitalism.

- **Trade unions** were defunded or disbanded if they leaned too far left.
- **Socialist newspapers** lost advertisers and licenses.
- **Governments** were pressured to purge communist cabinet ministers, even in countries where they had been elected.

In Italy, U.S. diplomats funneled money to centrist parties, funded anti-communist propaganda, and threatened to withhold aid if the left won the 1948 elections (Kinzer 104).

This was not democracy in action.

This was **democracy managed** with American capital as both a carrot and a stick.

Case Study: Greece, Bullets and Bread

Greece became one of the earliest battlegrounds of this "economic diplomacy." After World War II, a civil war broke out between the Western-backed government and leftist resistance fighters, many of whom had led anti-Nazi efforts during the war.

Rather than allow the Greek people to determine their postwar future, the U.S. funneled weapons, advisors, and economic aid to the monarchy, enabling mass executions, torture, and the silencing of opposition.

What was billed as "support for freedom" became a **green light for state violence**, so long as the recipient pledged loyalty to Washington.

The Economic Boomerang

While European economies did recover, helped along by the $13 billion in U.S. aid (equivalent to over $160 billion today), the plan also **restructured global capitalism** in America's favor.

- European industry became dependent on U.S. goods, credit, and technology.
- American corporations gained access to new markets and labor.
- The dollar solidified its role as the dominant global currency.

As historian Tony Judt noted, "The Marshall Plan did not just rebuild Europe, it rebuilt it in America's image" (*Postwar* 91).

What began as aid ended as **alignment**. What was framed as solidarity functioned as a form of **hegemony**.

The Myth Lives On

To this day, the Marshall Plan is held up as a moment of U.S. moral greatness, a selfless act of global stewardship. It is taught in textbooks, praised by politicians, and repeated in policy circles as the gold standard of "democracy promotion."

However, for many in the Global South, and even parts of Europe, the lesson is different:

Be grateful but stay in line.

Accept aid but relinquish autonomy.

Choose democracy, but only the **American version**, or risk being labeled unstable, radical, or undemocratic.

Conclusion: Generosity or Geopolitics?

The Marshall Plan was not a lie, but it was **never the whole truth**. It was rebuilt, yes. However, it also rebranded power, securing America's place at the top of a global economic order that prized markets over movements and obedience over independence.

It was the beginning of a new era when democracy became a product, and the United States became its **exclusive distributor**.

The lion's roar now echoed through banks, trade agreements, and foreign ministries.
It didn't need to conquer. It had loans, blueprints, and the myth of benevolence.

Works Cited

Judt, Tony. *Postwar: A History of Europe Since 1945*. Penguin Press, 2005.

Kinzer, Stephen. *Overthrow: America's Century of Regime Change from Hawaii to Iraq*. Henry Holt, 2006.

Westad, Odd Arne. *The Global Cold War: Third World Interventions and the Making of Our Times*. Cambridge University Press, 2005.

Hogan, Michael J. *The Marshall Plan: America, Britain, and the Reconstruction of Western Europe, 1947–1952*. Cambridge University Press, 1987.

Leffler, Melvyn P. *A Preponderance of Power: National Security, the Truman Administration, and the Cold War*. Stanford University Press, 1992.

III. Democracy at Gunpoint, Military Interventions and Puppet Regimes

Elections with an Exit Wound

For all its talk of freedom, America has an unsettling habit: when people abroad choose leaders the United States does not like, the ballot box suddenly becomes a threat, not a triumph. Moreover, democracy, the very thing Washington claims to defend, is treated like a fire to be extinguished.

This is the darker truth behind decades of U.S. foreign policy: that democracy has too often been spread **at the barrel of a gun**, imposed through coups, airstrikes, assassinations, and covert operations. Furthermore, those on the receiving end were not liberated. They were **broken**, their sovereignty dismantled, their economies hijacked, their futures rewritten to fit Washington's script.

This was not an accident.

It was disguised as defense, justified through ideology, and always, always branded as freedom.

Iran, 1953: The Coup that Shaped the Century

Mohammad Mossadegh was not a terrorist. He was not a warlord or a strongman. He was a democratically elected prime minister, chosen by the Iranian people in 1951. His "crime"? Nationalizing Iran's oil industry, which had long been dominated by the British-owned Anglo-Iranian Oil Company (later BP).

When Mossadegh moved to take control of Iran's natural resources and use the profits to invest in public services, the response was swift and brutal. The CIA, in collaboration with British intelligence, orchestrated **Operation Ajax**, a covert coup that overthrew Mossadegh and reinstalled the Shah, an authoritarian monarch more amenable to Western oil interests.

What followed was **25 years of repression**, secret police terror, censorship, and U.S.-backed rule, until the 1979 Islamic Revolution exploded in response.

This was the price of democracy denied: a society traumatized, radicalized, and plunged into decades of unrest.

Guatemala, 1954: Agrarian Reform Meets American Empire

In Guatemala, President Jacobo Árbenz attempted something radical: he sought to redistribute land to the people. Under his administration, the government enacted agrarian reform to redistribute uncultivated land from large foreign corporations, including the powerful **United Fruit Company**, which had close ties to top U.S. officials.

Fearing the spread of socialism (and the loss of profits), the Eisenhower administration branded Árbenz a communist threat. The CIA launched **Operation PBSUCCESS**, funding militias, dropping propaganda leaflets, and installing a military junta after Árbenz was forced to resign.

The result? **A 36-year civil war** that left more than 200,000 dead, many of them Indigenous villagers massacred in scorched-earth campaigns.

In the name of democracy, the United States buried it.

Chile, 1973: The Death of a Dream

Salvador Allende became the world's first Marxist president elected through democratic means. He came to power with promises of land reform, nationalization of copper (Chile's lifeblood), and healthcare expansion. However, from the outset, he faced sabotage, not from his people, but from abroad.

Declassified documents reveal that the Nixon administration and Henry Kissinger viewed Allende's election not as a democratic success, but as a crisis. CIA funds flowed into opposition parties, media outlets, and eventually to the Chilean military.

On September 11, 1973, the Chilean military launched a coup. Allende was killed in the presidential palace. Thousands were arrested, tortured, or disappeared under General Augusto Pinochet's dictatorship, which ruled for nearly two decades, with full U.S. support.

The United States toppled democracy to protect capitalism. Moreover, it referred to the operation as a defense of freedom.

The Blueprint: Destroy First, Install Later

Across the Global South, the pattern repeated:

- In Congo, the U.S. helped assassinate Patrice Lumumba, a charismatic anti-colonial leader, only to replace him with Mobutu Sese Seko, one of the most corrupt despots of the 20th century.
- In **Vietnam**, the U.S. undermined peace talks, propped up authoritarian leaders, and escalated into a full-blown war that left millions dead.
- In **Nicaragua**, **El Salvador**, **Honduras**, and **Panama**, U.S.-backed regimes tortured, executed, and disappeared thousands, all while being hailed in Washington as bulwarks against communism.

These were not failures of democracy.

They were deliberate choices to **sacrifice it for geopolitical gain**.

The Cost of "Liberation"

In nearly every case, American intervention created more instability than it solved:

- Countries were left with weak institutions, fractured societies, and long memories of betrayal.
- Resistance movements were pushed underground, often radicalized by repression.
- Generations grew up equating "democracy" not with justice, but with **tanks, torture, and traitors in expensive suits**.

However, American leaders continued to insist: *We are bringing freedom.*

However, freedom imposed at gunpoint isn't freedom. It is a theater. It is not a democracy. It is domination disguised as electoral politics.

Conclusion: The Silent Graveyard of Sovereignty

The United States has claimed to be the guardian of democracy. In Iran, Chile, Guatemala, and dozens of other nations, it became its **undertaker**.

The ballots burned. The voices were silent. The dreams assassinated.

And for what? Markets? Minerals? Fear of another ideology rising?

The lion roared across the globe, promising to protect. In the rubble it left behind, the world learned the truth:
That democracy, when sold as a weapon, **leaves no one free**.

Works Cited

Kinzer, Stephen. *Overthrow: America's Century of Regime Change from Hawaii to Iraq*. Henry Holt, 2006.

Gleijeses, Piero. *Shattered Hope: The Guatemalan Revolution and the United States, 1944–1954*. Princeton University Press, 1991.

Grandin, Greg. *The Last Colonial Massacre: Latin America in the Cold War*. University of Chicago Press, 2004.

Westad, Odd Arne. *The Global Cold War: Third World Interventions and the Making of Our Times*. Cambridge University Press, 2005.

Harmer, Tanya. *Allende's Chile and the Inter-American Cold War*. University of North Carolina Press, 2011.

IV. The Weaponization of "Free and Fair" Elections

Vote How We Like, or Else

Democracy, we are told, begins at the ballot box. It is sacred, universal, the voice of the people rising to shape their destiny. However, what happens when that voice chooses something Washington disapproves of?

In theory, the United States celebrates elections as the hallmark of freedom. In practice, it has too often treated them like a **litmus test for loyalty**, validating the results only if the winners are ideologically aligned, economically obedient, and politically convenient.

When the people vote "correctly," it is democracy.

When they do not, it becomes a “crisis,” a “mistake,” a “threat to regional stability.”

Moreover, suddenly, the very system America claims to champion is **undermined, overruled, or quietly dismantled**.

This is not democracy promotion.

It is democracy **policing**, dressed up as diplomacy.

The Double Standard of Democracy

From the Cold War through the War on Terror, U.S. support for elections has followed a simple rule: if the outcome helps preserve U.S. interests, politically, militarily, or economically, it is celebrated. If not, it is delegitimized, sanctioned, or overthrown.

Elections have become **tests of submission**, not expressions of sovereignty.

Consider two scenarios:

- A pro-Western leader wins a flawed election riddled with corruption and voter suppression, the U.S. calls it a “step forward for democracy.”
- A leftist or nationalist leader wins a transparent, widely monitored election, the U.S. calls it “concerning” or “destabilizing,” often followed by sanctions, isolation, or regime change efforts.

The ballot box, then, is not a tool for people. It is a **barometer for Washington’s approval**.

Case Study: Haiti, The President Who Was Elected Twice and Ousted Twice

Jean-Bertrand Aristide, a former Catholic priest and advocate for the poor, won Haiti's 1990 election with overwhelming popular support. He promised land reform, human rights, and an end to elite corruption. However, for the U.S. and Haiti's entrenched oligarchy, his agenda was too radical.

Within months, he was overthrown in a military coup. Though briefly restored in 1994 under U.S. pressure, primarily to maintain order rather than support his policies, Aristide was again **removed in 2004** under murky circumstances involving international pressure and U.S. intervention.

Twice elected. Twice ousted. The people will be dismissed both times in the name of "stability."

Case Study: Palestine, Democracy Denied

In 2006, Palestinians in Gaza and the West Bank voted in a legislative election widely considered **free and fair** by international observers. Hamas, running on a platform of social services and resistance to occupation, won a majority of seats.

The response from Washington and its allies?

Immediate rejection of the results, economic sanctions, and the suspension of aid.

The justification? Hamas was considered a terrorist organization, and its victory could not be allowed to stand, even though **the people had spoken**.

In Palestine, democracy was supported only when it voted for the "right" side.

The ballot box was sacred until it became inconvenient.

Case Study: Ukraine, Selective Support, Strategic Silence

The 2004 Ukrainian presidential election sparked the **Orange Revolution**, characterized by massive protests that alleged electoral fraud. The U.S. supported the opposition, funded civil society groups, and used media channels to amplify dissent, all in the name of defending democracy.

In 2014, following the ousting of a pro-Russian president, the new Ukrainian government aligned with the West and accepted significant support from NATO and the EU.

However, in other contexts, when pro-Western regimes suppress opposition or silence dissent, **the U.S. rarely intervenes**.

The message is clear: democracy is valid only when it **leans westward**.

The Tools of Electoral Control

Democracy promotion is not just about funding ballots and monitoring polling stations. It is a **full-spectrum influence campaign**, with tactics that include:

- **Training opposition parties** through U.S.-funded NGOs.
- **Shaping media narratives** through embassies and strategic messaging.
- **Funding civil society** selectively, favoring groups aligned with neoliberal or pro-Western values.
- **Sanctioning or isolating governments** whose electoral outcomes are politically undesirable.

These tactics create a tilted playing field, where the people may cast votes, but **external forces have already curated the menu of options**.

The Illusion of Neutrality

The U.S. presents itself as an impartial referee of global democracy, a mentor guiding fragile nations through the growing pains of political maturity.

However, in practice, it behaves more like a coach rigging the match, handing the ball to favored players, rewriting the rules mid-game, and ejecting any team that challenges its authority.

Furthermore, when the scoreboard does not favor its interests, it simply declares the game invalid.

Conclusion: When the Ballot Box Becomes a Battlefield

Free and fair elections are supposed to be the heartbeat of democracy. However, for too many nations, that heartbeat is manipulated, engineered to beat in rhythm with foreign power.

Elections become spectacles. Voters become pawns. Moreover, democracy becomes an illusion, not because the people do not believe in it, but because **they are not allowed to define it for themselves**.

The lion still roars about "supporting democratic transitions."

Nevertheless, behind the roar is a whisper: *Choose what we choose, or your vote does not count.*

Works Cited

Chomsky, Noam. *Hegemony or Survival: America's Quest for Global Dominance*. Metropolitan Books, 2003.

Falk, Richard. *The Declining World Order: America's Imperial Geopolitics*. Routledge, 2004.

Kirkpatrick, Jeane. "Dictatorships and Double Standards." *Commentary Magazine*, 1979.

Brown, Stephen. *Transnational Democracy Promotion and Resistance.* Routledge, 2013.

The Carter Center. *Observations on the Palestinian Legislative Elections*, 2006.

Hallward, Peter. *Damming the Flood: Haiti, Aristide, and the Politics of Containment*. Verso Books, 2007.

V. Hollywood, Academia, and the Cultural Machinery of Influence

Democracy as Entertainment, America as Savior

If tanks, coups, and ballots were the complex tools of America's global influence, then culture was its soft weapon, and perhaps its most potent.

After World War II, while Soviet tanks rolled through Eastern Europe, American films rolled into cinemas across Africa, Asia, and Latin America. Pop songs drowned out revolutionary anthems. Ivy League scholarships replaced anti-colonial tracts. Moreover, sitcoms, superhero franchises, and glamorous war movies subtly conveyed a message to the world: **freedom looks like America.**

This was not just an accidental influence.

It was **deliberate design**, a cultural doctrine embedded in diplomacy, media, and education, where the U.S. positioned itself not just as a global leader, but as **the moral center of civilization**.

The result? A generation of postcolonial minds was raised on the belief that democracy was represented by white picket fences, military heroism, Wall Street prosperity, and red, white, and blue salvation.

Hollywood: The Dream Factory with a Flag

From *Casablanca* to *Captain America*, Hollywood has long been a stage where U.S. foreign policy quietly rehearses its narratives. Villains wear turbans or Eastern European accents. Heroes parachute into the Global South to save the helpless. The CIA becomes sexy. The military gets redemption arcs. Moreover, revolutionaries are framed as dangerous, unstable, or naïve.

This is not just storytelling. It is **statecraft** in real time.

- During the Cold War, the U.S. government collaborated closely with studios to produce anti-communist films that were shown in American-allied nations.

- The Pentagon regularly funds, censors, and provides resources for films that portray the military positively, from *Top Gun* to *Zero Dark Thirty*.
- Characters in blockbusters rarely question capitalism, empire, or white Western saviors. When they do, they are killed off, redeemed, or marginalized.

The camera does not just capture America. It choreographs its moral superiority.

Case Study: Africa on Screen

In most mainstream films set in Africa, the story is rarely told from an African perspective. The continent becomes a backdrop, a place of disease, war, and chaos, waiting for the white doctor, soldier, or journalist to arrive and impose order.

- In *The Last King of Scotland*, a white Scottish doctor becomes the moral anchor in Idi Amin's Uganda.
- In *Blood Diamond*, the Sierra Leone conflict is framed around Leonardo DiCaprio's redemption arc.
- Even in *Hotel Rwanda*, the focus shifts away from African resistance to Western bureaucratic failure.

Rarely do African heroes lead. Rarely do Western powers bear responsibility for the chaos they left behind.

Colonialism disappears, and Hollywood fills the void with tropes.

Academia: The Factory of Ideological Consent

U.S. universities, think tanks, and exchange programs have also played a quiet role in exporting American democratic ideology.

- **Fulbright scholarships**, USAID fellowships, and State Department-funded programs bring foreign students to the U.S. for "leadership training", reinforcing neoliberal economics, individualism, and U.S.-friendly politics.

- **Political science curricula** around the world were restructured after the Cold War to prioritize American models of governance, with Western textbooks dominating classrooms from Ghana to Jordan.
- **Think tanks** like the National Endowment for Democracy (NED) and the American Enterprise Institute promote free markets and regime change under the guise of research and "civil society support."

The result? Local elites educated in American universities return home fluent in U.S. foreign policy preferences, often rising to power with a worldview that places **America at the center and their traditions on the margins**.

The mind was colonized long before the military ever arrived.

Soft Power as Strategic Engineering

Joseph Nye, the political scientist who coined the term "soft power," described it as the ability to **shape the preferences of others through appeal and attraction** rather than coercion. However, what he did not fully confront was how deeply manipulative that appeal can become when billions of dollars in media, philanthropy, and educational infrastructure back it.

Soft power is not neutral. It is **hierarchical**.

It teaches the world that:

- Liberation looks like American capitalism.
- Progress looks like English-speaking technocrats.
- Modernity looks like shedding your indigenous values in favor of Western rationalism.

Moreover, those who resist this narrative. They are called backward. Dangerous. Unstable. Undemocratic.

Cultural Control in the Global South

In the post-independence period, many nations attempted to build their democratic systems rooted in traditional governance, socialism, or religious ethics. However, these experiments were often undermined not by guns, but by cultural factors.

- African socialism was ridiculed as corrupt and naïve.
- Islamic democracy was cast as inherently theocratic and oppressive.
- Latin American populism was reframed as authoritarian chaos.

Meanwhile, U.S.-backed media outlets, from *Voice of America* to *Radio Free Europe*, blanketed the globe with narratives that equated "freedom" with U.S. influence and painted resistance as failure.

Conclusion: Who Tells the Story, Owns the World

American democracy did not just spread through wars or aid. It spread through **narratives**, through cameras, scholarships, syllabi, and songs.

It became the air people breathed, even when they choked on it.

Moreover, in that air, alternative democratic dreams suffocated. Voices from the margins were drowned out by billion-dollar blockbusters, Ivy League endorsements, and the seductive lie that to be free is to be like America.

The lion's roar reached through radio waves, film reels, and textbooks.

Nevertheless, what it silenced was more potent than what it preached.

Works Cited

Nye, Joseph S. *Soft Power: The Means to Success in World Politics*. Public Affairs, 2004.

Said, Edward. *Culture and Imperialism*. Vintage Books, 1994.

Schiller, Herbert. *Communication and Cultural Domination*. M.E.

Sharpe, 1976.

Mazrui, Ali A. *The African Condition: A Political Diagnosis*. Heinemann, 1980.

Curtis, Devon. "The Limits of Soft Power in Africa." *International Affairs*, vol. 84, no. 6, 2008, pp. 1009–1025.

VI. The Economics of Democratic Conversion

Vote First, Starve Later

When American officials spoke of spreading democracy, they rarely mentioned what came next.

They did not mention the **contracts**, the **austerity measures**, the **corporate handshakes** sealed behind closed doors. They did not say that voting was often followed by privatization, or that "freedom" came tied to loans with interest rates that bled nations dry.

Because democracy, at least the version the United States exported, was not just political. It was **economic ideology wrapped in a ballot box**.

It promised the right to vote but demanded allegiance to **free-market orthodoxy**.
It gave you elections but stripped your state of the power to feed, heal, or educate its people.

This is the quiet violence of what came to be known as **the neoliberal** system that masqueraded as reform but functioned as recolonization.

Democracy with a Balance Sheet

Throughout the 1980s and 1990s, dozens of nations in the Global South, newly independent and struggling to find their footing, were told by the West that prosperity required structural change. The script was familiar:

Open your markets.

Deregulate your industries.
Cut social spending.
Furthermore, most of all, **privatize**.

These demands were not suggestions. They were **conditions** set by the World Bank, the International Monetary Fund (IMF), and U.S. agencies on which aid, loans, and diplomatic legitimacy depended.

Democracy became **a pay-to-play system**.

Furthermore, sovereignty became the first casualty.

Case Study: Zambia, The Cost of Compliance

In the early 1990s, Zambia transitioned from one-party rule to multiparty democracy under Western encouragement. In exchange, the IMF and World Bank offered loan packages and "development guidance." However, that guidance came at a steep cost:

- State-run industries were dismantled.
- Thousands of public workers were laid off.
- Health and education budgets were gutted.
- Foreign investors were invited to take control of Zambia's rich copper resources, its economic lifeline.

The people voted, but **their government no longer controlled their economy**.

The flag changed. The anthem played. However, the levers of power had moved elsewhere.

Today, Zambia's debt crisis has worsened, and the "democracy" it was sold has left millions trapped in poverty, with no safety net and no say in the economic system that governs their lives.

From Sovereignty to Submission

Across the Global South, this pattern became all too familiar:

- **Ghana** slashed food subsidies under IMF pressure, leading to mass protests and hunger.
- **Jamaica** opened its markets to American milk powder, collapsing its local dairy industry.
- **Argentina** privatized everything from water to pensions, then watched its economy collapse in 2001, leaving millions unemployed and impoverished.

These were not isolated incidents. They were part of a coordinated strategy: use debt as leverage to force democratic governments to abandon public welfare and embrace **market fundamentalism**.

The right to vote was never enough. Because what is democracy without the power to decide your economic path?

Economic Shock Therapy Disguised as Reform

This model became known as the **Washington Consensus**, a set of ten policy prescriptions promoted by the U.S. Treasury, the IMF, and the World Bank, framed as "best practices" for developing democracies.

However, behind the polite language of "liberalization" and "good governance" was a brutal reality:

- Public services were sold to private firms.
- Education became a privilege.
- Water, electricity, and healthcare turned into commodities.
- And foreign corporations reaped profits while domestic industries died.

All in the name of freedom.

All under the banner of democratic transition.

Case Study: Russia's Ruined Transition

After the fall of the Soviet Union, the U.S. and the IMF rushed into Russia with promises of rapid democratization and economic rebirth.

What followed was a disaster:

- State assets were auctioned off to oligarchs.
- GDP collapsed.
- Life expectancy fell.
- A tiny elite got rich while tens of millions faced hunger and homelessness.

Democracy became a dirty word for many Russians, not because they opposed elections, but because what came with democracy was **poverty, corruption, and humiliation**.

Furthermore, the West called it progress.

The Human Cost: Debt, Dependency, and Despair

These economic "reforms" created a new kind of colonialism, one in which foreign banks, corporations, and institutions controlled the nation's lifeblood.

- **Debt servicing replaced development.**
- **Foreign approval replaced local planning.**
- **Budgets were written in Washington and imposed in Nairobi, Dhaka, and La Paz.**

Moreover, the people who voted, marched, and dreamed were told to wait. To tighten their belts. To be patient. Because democracy would bring growth.

Nevertheless, what kind of democracy tells mothers they cannot afford medicine for their children while corporations pay zero taxes on billion-dollar mineral contracts?

What kind of democracy forces teachers to strike for chalk while billionaires receive tax holidays?

Conclusion: The Freedom to Choose, But Only One Option

The United States did not just export democracy. It exported **an economic cage**, beautifully branded, heavily marketed, and enforced with loan agreements and diplomatic smiles.

People could vote, yes.

However, only for governments that agreed to sell their public wealth, silence their unions, and obey international markets.

In this version of democracy, the ballot is a leash.

Moreover, the lion still roars, not through armies, but through spreadsheets.

Works Cited

Klein, Naomi. *The Shock Doctrine: The Rise of Disaster Capitalism*. Picador, 2007.

Stiglitz, Joseph E. *Globalization and Its Discontents*. W.W. Norton & Company, 2002.

Mkandawire, Thandika. "Adjustment, Political Conditionality and Democratisation in Africa." *Nordic Journal of African Studies*, vol. 4, no. 2, 1995.

Rodrik, Dani. *The Globalization Paradox: Democracy and the Future of the World Economy*. W.W. Norton, 2011.

Peet, Richard. *Unholy Trinity: The IMF, World Bank, and WTO*. Zed Books, 2003.

VII. Democracy's Silent Exceptions: The Allies That Get a Pass

Freedom for Friends, Silence for Killers

In the official script of American diplomacy, democracy is a non-negotiable virtue. A guiding star. A condition of partnership. A sacred ideal to be protected at all costs.

Unless, of course, you are helpful.

Then democracy becomes negotiable.

Then repression becomes "internal affairs."

Then elections can be postponed, dissent silenced, protesters jailed, if you stay in line, keep the oil flowing, the contracts coming, and the rhetoric tame.

This is the unspoken rule of U.S. foreign policy: **it is not who governs that matters, but whom they serve**. A loyal tyrant will always be preferred to a disobedient democrat.

Freedom, it turns out, is not for everyone.

Some get the bombs.

Others get the blindfold.

Saudi Arabia: Absolute Monarchy, Absolute Silence

Saudi Arabia is not a democracy. It has no elected parliament. No freedom of speech. No political parties. No equal rights for women. Dissent is a criminal offense. Bloggers are lashed. Dissidents have disappeared. Executions are public.

However, for decades, the United States has treated the Saudi monarchy as a cornerstone of "regional stability."

Why?

- It controls the world's largest oil reserves.
- It buys billions in U.S. weapons.
- It helps contain Iran, America's main regional rival.

So, when journalist **Jamal Khashoggi** was murdered and dismembered inside the Saudi consulate in Turkey in 2018, the U.S. response was muted. There was no regime change talk. No sanctions on oil. No lectures about human rights.

The lion purred instead of roaring, because the butcher was a business partner.

Egypt: From Revolution to Repression

After the 2011 Arab Spring uprising toppled Hosni Mubarak, Egypt held its first free election. However, when Mohamed Morsi, a Muslim Brotherhood candidate, won the presidency, he lasted just one year before being ousted by a military coup.

General Abdel Fattah el-Sisi took over, imprisoning tens of thousands, outlawing opposition parties, and cracking down on civil society.

The U.S. referred to it as a "transition."

It resumed aid within months.

Why?

- Egypt is a key ally in the Israel-Palestine conflict.
- It secures the Suez Canal, a vital trade route.
- It supports U.S. counterterrorism objectives in the region.

Democracy died on camera in Tahrir Square. Washington sent more funding.

Israel: Democracy with Checkpoints

Israel is often praised as "the only democracy in the Middle East." Moreover, in many respects, robust elections, an independent judiciary, and a free press meet many democratic standards.

Only for some.

For millions of Palestinians living under military occupation in the West Bank and siege in Gaza, democracy is a wall they are not allowed to climb. Their land is expropriated. Their movements are restricted. Their children were arrested. Their homes were demolished.

Human rights groups, including Amnesty International, Human Rights Watch, and Israel's own B'Tselem, have labeled the system **apartheid**.

However, U.S. officials repeat the refrain: "Unbreakable bond." No matter how many UN resolutions are ignored. No matter how many civilians are killed. No matter how loud the global outrage becomes.

The lion roars for democracy, but whispers when it comes to its favored child.

The Pattern: Repression with Perks

This double standard extends beyond the Middle East:

- **Rwanda**: Authoritarian rule is tolerated because of its role in regional security and genocide prevention.
- **Colombia**: Death squads were overlooked during its drug war partnership with the U.S.
- **Turkey**: Crackdowns on media, Kurdish communities, and opposition parties downplayed due to its NATO membership.

These are not anomalies. They are **features** of a policy framework that defines democracy not by its values, but by its **utility**.

What "Strategic Partnership" Really Means

In U.S. foreign policy, "strategic partner" is often code for:

"You may kill, jail, censor, or disappear your people, as long as you buy our weapons, oppose our enemies, and say the right things at the UN."

This kind of democracy is not built on principle.

It is built on **contracts**.

Furthermore, the price is paid by journalists, activists, indigenous leaders, opposition parties, and the invisible millions who live under regimes **shielded by America's silence**.

Conclusion: The Moral Cost of Selective Outrage

American foreign policy often emphasizes the importance of values. However, it goes through **calculated exceptions**. Moreover, every time it props up a dictator, funds a regime, or excuses a massacre, it teaches the world a bitter lesson:

That democracy is not a human right. It is a **weapon**, selectively deployed.
That some lives are disposable. That some voters do not matter. That some nations will never be allowed to choose for themselves.

The lion still claims to defend democracy. Nevertheless, it only bares its teeth for the disobedient.

For the rest, it turns its gaze, cashes the check, and walks away.

Works Cited

Kaye, Dalia Dassa. *A Middle East Free of Weapons of Mass Destruction: A New Approach to Nonproliferation*. Routledge, 2012.

Brownlee, Jason. *Authoritarianism in an Age of Democratization*. Cambridge University Press, 2007.

Human Rights Watch. *World Report 2023: Events of 2022*. HRW, 2023.
B'Tselem. *A Regime of Jewish Supremacy from the Jordan River to the Mediterranean Sea: This Is Apartheid*. B'Tselem, 2021.

Riedel, Bruce. *Kings and Presidents: Saudi Arabia and the United States since FDR*. Brookings Institution Press,

VIII. Resistance from the Margins: The Dream Rejected

Not in Our Name

For every coup installed, there was a movement that refused to die. For every election manipulated, some people stood tall. For every handout of democracy tied with strings, there was a voice from the margins that said: *No, not like this.*

This section is not about victimhood. It is about resistance. It is about the leaders, movements, and everyday citizens who **saw through the façade**, who understood that democracy, when delivered in American packaging, often came with **a leash**.

They accepted democracy. They rejected **domination disguised as freedom**.
They dreamed of dignity, not dependency. Of governance rooted in tradition, language, land, and justice, not in Washington's checklist.

Their resistance was punished. Silenced. Sanctioned and sometimes assassinated.

However, it still endured.

Cuba: Building a Revolution in the Shadow of a Superpower

In 1959, Fidel Castro led a successful revolution that overthrew U.S.-backed dictator Fulgencio Batista. The new Cuban government declared itself independent, not just in name, but in economic policy, land ownership, and foreign alliances.

- U.S. corporations were nationalized.
- Healthcare and education were made universal.
- The island aligned itself with anti-imperial struggles across Africa and Latin America.

The response?

A U.S. embargo that has lasted over six decades.

Invasions. Assassination attempts. Diplomatic isolation.

Cuba's version of democracy, flawed, imperfect, and deeply contested, was never allowed to stand as a viable alternative because **it proved that another model was possible**.

Palestine: When Voting Became a Crime

In 2006, Palestinians held legislative elections under the supervision of international observers. The result? A landslide victory for Hamas, a political and social movement that had provided services and resisted occupation but was also designated as a terrorist organization by the U.S. and its allies.

The people had spoken.

Washington refused to listen.

- Aid was cut.
- Gaza was blockaded.
- The elected government was isolated.

Democracy was only respected if it bowed to Israel and the West. A free vote became a geopolitical sin.

In Palestine, resistance was not just in stone-throwing or slogans. It was in the belief that their voice mattered, even when the world refused to hear it.

Venezuela: Elections, Oil, and the Price of Defiance

When Hugo Chávez was elected president of Venezuela in 1998, he achieved this with overwhelming popular support, particularly among the poor and working class. He redistributed oil wealth, expanded healthcare and education, and challenged U.S. dominance in the region.

The reaction from Washington was swift and predictable:

- A failed coup in 2002 that the U.S. tacitly supported.

- Decades of sanctions aimed at crippling the economy.
- Media demonization of Venezuela as a failed state, even when its elections remained competitive and widely observed.

Chávez and, later, Maduro were not punished for authoritarianism. They were punished for **disobedience**.

Africa: The Reawakening of Sovereignty

In the 21st century, African nations began to push back against externally imposed models of governance. Leaders such as Thomas Sankara, Muammar Gaddafi (before his political shift), and Kwame Nkrumah advocated for **Pan-African unity**, economic independence, and cultural revival.

Their visions challenged not just colonialism, but **neo-colonialism**, the control of African states through aid, debt, and "democratic" prescriptions from abroad.

Most were toppled, killed, or isolated.

Today, new resistance is emerging, from Niger to Mali to Burkina Faso, where military leaders and civil movements are rejecting French and U.S. influence in favor of **indigenous models of governance**, regional cooperation, and multipolar alliances, such as BRICS.

These are not coups for power's sake. They are **a product** of generations who refuse to live under economic servitude cloaked in ballots and buzzwords.

What They Wanted

These resisters didn't oppose democracy.

They opposed the democracy that came with:

- Airstrikes and oil contracts
- IMF debt and surveillance bases
- CIA-backed NGOs and Western media narratives

- Ballot boxes with one approved candidate

They wanted self-determination.

Not sermons.

They wanted solidarity.

Not sanctions.

They wanted a democracy that could wear **their face**, not one carved in stone 4,000 miles away.

Conclusion: The Right to Refuse

In every corner of the world, from Havana to Harare, Gaza to Caracas, there have always been those who refused to kneel, who said:

"We will govern ourselves. We will make mistakes. We will learn. However, we will not wear your chains and call it choice."

The lion claimed to bring democracy. Nevertheless, many gazelles saw the claws beneath the handshake.
They rejected the dream not because they feared freedom, but because they knew absolute freedom cannot be imported. It must be **built from the soil up**, in the language of the people, for the people.

Moreover, that, perhaps, is what frightened the lion most.

Works Cited

Chomsky, Noam. *Failed States: The Abuse of Power and the Assault on Democracy*. Metropolitan Books, 2006.

Gott, Richard. *Cuba: A New History*. Yale University Press, 2005.

Hallward, Peter. *Damming the Flood: Haiti, Aristide, and the Politics of Containment*. Verso, 2007.

Prashad, Vijay. *The Poorer Nations: A Possible History of the Global South*. Verso, 2013.

Ajayi, J. F. Ade. *A Patriot to the Core: Selected Speeches of Kwame Nkrumah*. African Institute of Leadership, 2010.

IX. A Dream Deferred, A Mask Removed

What Remains After the Flags Are Folded

For decades, the United States has stood before the world draped in stars and stripes, waving the banner of democracy like a gospel. It promised nations a future if they followed its lead, elections, markets, freedom, and progress. It told them that it was *the* way. That it was a form of democracy was not just ideal, it was **inevitable**.

Moreover, for a time, the world tried to believe it.

People danced in the streets after dictators fell. Aid flowed in. Training programs were launched. Ballot boxes were delivered by UN trucks. The dream felt real.

Nevertheless, slowly, painfully, reality intruded.

The flags came, but so did the loans, the surveillance, the foreign consultants, the privatization mandates. The tanks rolled in before the textbooks. The bombs dropped before the ballots. The cameras filmed only what Washington wanted to remember.

Moreover, the people in Guatemala, Iran, Congo, Vietnam, Chile, Palestine, Venezuela, Libya, and beyond learned that democracy, when delivered in American packaging, often arrived with **a price tag and a target**.

The ballot became a branding tool.

The constitution became a leash.

The people will become negotiable if it does not serve the empire.

The Mask Slips

What happens when the dream starts to rot?

What happens when communities, once promised freedom to begin to see through the speeches and slogans?

- They see Haiti's elections, undermined and erased.
- They see Gaza's votes punished and starved.
- They see Congo's minerals extracted by Western companies while their roads remain unpaved.
- They see "democracy promotion" that funds militias and "civil society development" that topples sovereign governments.

They see a mask. Moreover, they know it is a mask.

Because freedom that silences you is not freedom.

Democracy that disciplines your vote is not democracy.

Aid that demands your obedience is not help. It is **control**.

The Aftermath: The Silence That Follows the Roar

When the coups end and the ballots are cast, when the tanks leave and the logos fade, what remains?

- Broken economies.
- Disillusioned youth.
- Burned libraries and censored textbooks.
- Culture made to feel small.
- Generations who grow up equating "democracy" with **betrayal**.

Furthermore, perhaps worst of all, a silence-a collective doubt in the very concept of self-rule, poisoned by years of false promises and forced policies.

That is the legacy of exporting democracy like Coca-Cola.

What Could Have Been

Imagine if the U.S. had supported genuine self-determination, not just for allies, but for all.

Imagine if democracy meant building **with**, not dictating **to**.

- Supporting Venezuela's right to control its oil.
- Allowing Iran to nationalize its resources without a coup.
- Letting Palestinians speak without starving them for it.
- Funding healthcare, not just security cooperation.
- Listening, truly listening to what democracy looks like in languages beyond English.

It could have been different.

It still can be.

Conclusion: Reclaiming the Word, Restoring the Meaning

This chapter is not written in bitterness. It is written in the grief of stolen potential, in the name of people whose dreams were trampled by powers that claimed to elevate them.

It is also written in hope.

Across the world, from Burkina Faso to Bolivia, Gaza to Guyana, voices are rising again, demanding not American democracy, but **authentic democracy**. Democracy that grows from the soil, that reflects the rhythm of the people, that does not fear its citizens.

Democracy cannot be exported.

It must be **cultivated, nurtured, protected, and most of all, chosen**.

Moreover, as the mask of U.S. exceptionalism slips further, the world is waking up. The lion's roar no longer stuns the jungle. Now, it startsles itself.

Works Cited

Chomsky, Noam. *Hegemony or Survival: America's Quest for Global Dominance*. Metropolitan Books, 2003.

Prashad, Vijay. *The Darker Nations: A People's History of the Third World*. The New Press, 2008.

Mamdani, Mahmood. *Good Muslim, Bad Muslim: America, the Cold War, and the Roots of Terror*. Pantheon Books, 2004.

Grandin, Greg. *Empire's Workshop: Latin America, the United States, and the Rise of the New Imperialism*. Metropolitan Books, 2006.

Falk, Richard. *Power Shift: On the New Global Order*. Zed Books, 2016.

Chapter 4:

Beneath the Mane, Democracy as a Cover for Empire

The Language of Liberty, the Machinery of Domination

Chapter Theme

This chapter does not begin with outrage; it starts with grief.

Grief for the peoples and nations that believed in democracy, only to find themselves occupied, indebted, surveilled, or bombarded by the very country that claimed to bring it. Grief for the word itself, *democracy*, which once meant self-determination, but now too often arrives wrapped in camouflage netting and aid packages with fine print.

In the story, the U.S. tells the world that democracy is its gift, a noble, generous, and indispensable one. However, in the story history, democracy has also been a **costume**, a soft cloak draped over the cold machinery of empire. It has been the language used to sell invasions, justify coups, defend tyrants, erase local traditions, extract resources, and **discipline dissent**, all while promising freedom.

This chapter is not an indictment of democracy as an idea. It is a confrontation with how that idea was **bent into a weapon**.

We are not asking whether America failed to live up to its values. We are asking how **those values were engineered to serve power**, how freedom became a currency traded for loyalty, how elections became marketing campaigns for neoliberalism, how human rights became a selective hammer used to punish enemies while shielding friends.

This is not a chapter about broken promises.

It is a chapter about promises never meant to be kept.

We will follow the footprints left by "democracy promotion", into the rubble of Iraq, the streets of Cairo, the jungles of Nicaragua, and the boardrooms where aid, arms, and allegiance are negotiated. We will examine how military alliances with despots were framed as diplomacy, how war crimes were buried under soundbites about security, and how global institutions became instruments of Western consolidation.

This chapter asks not what went wrong, but **what was designed that way from the start**.

Because sometimes, the lion's name is not legal. It is camouflage.

Moreover, beneath it, you do not find liberty.

You find **control**.

I. Introduction: The Cloak of Empire

How Freedom Became a Sales Pitch for Power

There is something fierce about betrayal wrapped in virtue.

Empires of the past rarely pretended to be anything but what they were. Rome sent legions. Britain raised flags. Belgium used chains. America? America perfected a different kind of conquest, one that marched not under the banner of empire, but under the name of *liberation*: one that did not bring thrones or crowns, but constitutions and consultants.

One who learned to cloak domination in the language of **democracy**.

It did not appear to be a conquest. It looked like help. It did not sound like a threat. It sounded like a freedom speech.

Moreover, that is what made it so dangerous.

The Grand Illusion

Since the end of World War II, the United States has cast itself as a reluctant savior, a power that does not conquer but rescues, that does not colonize but guides, that does not dominate but *leads*. It has claimed, repeatedly, that it enters foreign lands not for profit, but to "restore order," to "spread freedom," to "build democracy."

However, scratch the surface of those claims, and the contradictions come roaring through.

- **How does a nation defend democracy while funding coups against elected leaders?**
- **How does it promote human rights while arming regimes that crush dissent with bullets and batons?**
- **How does it sell itself as a model of liberty while maintaining hundreds of military bases across the globe, many in places that never invited them?**

The answer is simple: it does not have to reconcile these contradictions; it only must **mask them**.

Furthermore, democracy is the mask.

Marketing Empire in the Language of Morality

This is not accidental. It is the architecture of modern imperialism: A blend of militarism, capitalism, and moral theater.

Where once power came with swords and soldiers, it now comes with **aid packages, trade deals, and press releases**. Where once resistance was crushed openly, it now dies quietly under economic sanctions, election interference, or NGO infiltration. Where once empires flaunted their conquest, America has learned to **frame it as service**.

This performance is seductive. Especially in a world that craves justice, fairness, and dignity. Especially for people who, after decades of colonial exploitation, still hunger for recognition and support.

Thus, when the lion roars, it does so not with claws bared, but with a speech on civil society, a televised summit on democratic values, a contract for privatizing public services dressed up as reform.

Beneath the mane, however, is the same old beast. Only better dressed.

More fluent. Moreover, it is far harder to see coming.

The Question This Chapter Asks

This chapter is not about whether American foreign policy has made mistakes. That framing is too generous, too forgiving, too easy.

This chapter asks a more complex question: **What if this is not about failure, but design?**

What if the goal was never to empower sovereign nations, but to **reshape them**?

Not to spread democracy, but to **engineer compliance**?

Not to liberate the oppressed, but to **manage their uprising** under new, Western-approved rules?

Moreover, what does it mean for the world, for Africa, for Latin America, for the Middle East, and Asia, when democracy is no longer a shared aspiration, but a **coded warning**?

The Stakes Are Real

This is not just theory. It is not just geopolitics. It is personal.

- It is the Afghan family who believed American promises and lost their home to a drone strike.
- It is the Congolese activist jailed after protesting a U.S.-backed mining deal.
- It is the Haitian voter whose president was removed by foreign pressure, twice.
- It is the Libyan child growing up among militias and rubble where a government once stood.

These are the people who live **beneath the mane**, not at the conference tables, not in policy briefs, but under the weight of an empire too proud to say its name.

Moreover, if we are to speak truth to power, then we must first name that power for what it is.

Conclusion: Pulling Back the Curtain

Before we examine the details, the coups dressed as interventions, the alliances with tyrants, the aid used as leverage, we must accept a sobering truth:

Democracy has become a brand. Furthermore, like all brands, it can be used to sell anything, even suffering.

This chapter strips away the branding. It follows the money, the missiles, the memoranda of understanding. It listens to the voices left out of press briefings and policy papers. It dares to ask: *What hides beneath the lion's mane?*

It is only when we confront the mask that we can begin to reclaim the meaning of freedom.

II. Democracy's Dual Face, Preacher and Enforcer

The Sermon on the Mount with a Drone in the Sky

The United States often speaks like a prophet.

It quotes Jefferson and Lincoln like scripture.

It lectures autocrats, bullies, and despots from global pulpits with the tone of a weary parent correcting a misbehaving child.

It preaches democracy.

Nevertheless, it enforces the empire.

Moreover, the world has noticed.

The Rhetoric of the Preacher

On any given day, you will hear U.S. officials condemn political repression in Venezuela, demand accountability in Cuba, or express "grave concern" over media censorship in Iran. The language is lofty, dressed in constitutional principle:

- "The right of the people to choose their leaders..."
- "Free and fair elections are the foundation of a free society..."
- "No one is above the law..."

These statements sound noble, and they echo the country's founding documents. However, they also conceal an uncomfortable reality:

The United States reserves its sermons only for its enemies.

When Saudi Arabia flogs activists, silence.

When Israel bombs journalists' homes, "Israel has the right to defend itself."

When Egypt jails 60,000 political prisoners, aid still flows.

When Colombia's security forces kill protesters, there is a diplomatic shrug.

This is not preaching. It's **performance**.

Furthermore, the message is clear: values are for export. They are not for everyone, and certainly not for allies.

The Machinery of the Enforcer

While the public hears the sermon, behind closed doors, and often in broad daylight, the enforcer goes to work:

- A shipment of tear gas for riot police in Nigeria.
- A drone strike in Somalia based on unverified intelligence.
- Economic sanctions that collapse entire healthcare systems in Syria or Venezuela.
- Surveillance training for militaries that monitor student movements and crush union organizers.

The U.S. does not just support global democracy. It **manages global**

dissent, deciding who may rise, who must be contained, and who can be tolerated for the time being.

This is a democracy with **surveillance contracts** and **military aid packages**.

It does not wear boots on the ground as often anymore. It does not need to. It has partners, drones, and a vast bureaucracy that **enforces order under the banner of freedom**.

Two Languages, One Policy

There are always two speeches. One for the cameras. One for the classified memos.

- Publicly: "We support the people of X in their pursuit of freedom."
- Privately: "Ensure the new government signs the trade agreement and aligns with NATO's strategic goals."

And in between these speeches? USAID funds civil society organizations through diplomatic visits by State Department advisors. The think tank reports calling for "democratic transitions" in resource-rich regions.

The U.S. is fluent in two tongues: the dialect of democracy and the language of leverage.

It speaks to the world. Moreover, it speaks to the other itself.

Case in Point: Tunisia, 2011–2023

After the Arab Spring, Tunisia was held up as a model, the only democracy to survive the wave of uprisings. U.S. officials praised the country's constitutional reforms, elections, and the vibrancy of its civil society.

However, when the government began jailing journalists and consolidating executive power in 2021, Washington hesitated. Why?

Tunisia remained **a strategic partner in counterterrorism** and hosted U.S. military cooperation in North Africa.

Freedom was important, but **not as important as stability**.

Not as important as the base.

Not as important as Tunisia staying in Washington's geopolitical orbit.

Global South's Growing Cynicism

People are paying attention.

From Lusaka to Lahore, from Port-au-Prince to Phnom Penh, people have watched American support swing wildly, not based on principle, but based on **strategic convenience**. Moreover, they have drawn their conclusions:

- That U.S.-style democracy comes with caveats.
- That the fundamental determination of friendship is obedience, not openness.
- That if you want to avoid sanctions or intervention, you must say the right things, but never actually **act** freely.

Democracy is the brand. However, **obedience is the product.**

Thus, many are turning elsewhere, to BRICS, to China, to regional coalitions that may not offer purity, but at least do not pretend.

Conclusion: The Split Mask

The United States does not wear one face, it wears two.

The preacher in public. The enforcer in private.

Moreover, the more the world hears the sermon while enduring suppression, the more it begins to see through the mask.

Because no matter how polished the speech, people remember the sanctions.

No matter how noble the promise, people remember the bombs.

Furthermore, no matter how often the lion roars about freedom, they remember the claws beneath the mane.

III. Regime Change in Righteous Language

Coups, Invasions, and Assassinations as "Democratic Interventions"

They call it liberation.

They call it restoring order.

Protecting civilians.

Promoting democracy.

When the smoke clears and the bodies are buried, the people left behind know what it really was: **invasion**, **occupation**, **assassination**, veiled in the soft language of human rights and the brutal tactics of war.

For decades, the United States has perfected the art of **toppling governments while claiming the moral high ground**. It does not need to declare an empire. It only needs to say it is "helping." And somehow, the coups are never called coups, the bombs are always precise, and the victims are always "collateral."

This is the theater of American democracy promotion, where regime change is the main act, and freedom is the costume.

The Playbook: How to Topple a Government in Five Steps

1. Declare the regime a threat to its people, to the region, to U.S. interests.
2. Frame the crisis in moral terms, talk of tyranny, suffering, and liberation.

3. Support opposition forces through funding, intelligence, and training.
4. Deploy covert action or military intervention, overt if possible, secret if necessary.
5. Install a client regime favorable to Western corporations, militaries, and markets.

It looks like democracy.
It sounds like democracy.

Nevertheless, it is **strategic obedience dressed as sovereignty**.

Case Study: Iraq (2003), Liberation or Looting?

In 2003, the Bush administration launched a full-scale invasion of Iraq under the justification that Saddam Hussein possessed weapons of mass destruction (WMDs) and posed an imminent threat.

There were no WMDs.

However, there was oil. And contracts. Moreover, billions in post-war reconstruction were tied to American firms.

The war was sold to the American public and the international community as an act of liberation, a mission to bring democracy to a people suffering under dictatorship.

The result?

- Over 500,000 Iraqis killed.
- Entire cities were destroyed.
- A government destabilized, leading to the rise of ISIS.
- A U.S.-installed regime haunted by corruption, sectarianism, and dependence.

Democracy did not arrive in Baghdad. Chaos did.

Moreover, from that chaos, American private contractors made a fortune.

Case Study: Libya (2011), The Humanitarian Bombing

In 2011, NATO, with U.S. backing launched a bombing campaign against Libya under the banner of "Responsibility to Protect" (R2P), claiming that Muammar Gaddafi was preparing to massacre civilians in Benghazi.

The campaign toppled the Libyan government within a matter of months.

Nevertheless, what followed was **not freedom**:

- Libya splintered into militia rule.
- Slave markets returned.
- Migrants drowned fleeing their shattered shores.
- U.S. weapons supplied to rebels ended up in jihadist hands.

Libya, which previously had the highest Human Development Index in Africa, has since become a failed state.

The West bombed the state but did not bother to build one. Furthermore, when the dust settled, there was no applause, only **ruin**.

Case Study: Chile (1973), When Democracy is Too Left-Wing

Salvador Allende, a Marxist doctor and reformist, was elected President of Chile in 1970, not by bullets, but by ballots. He promised land reform, the nationalization of copper (which had long been dominated by U.S. firms), and social equity.

The U.S. called him a threat to hemispheric security.

Documents now declassified show the CIA spent millions funding opposition media, sabotaging the economy, and plotting with the Chilean military.

On September 11, 1973, Allende was overthrown in a violent coup. He died in the presidential palace. His supporters were tortured, disappeared, or exiled.

The new regime?

General Augusto Pinochet, a brutal dictator who ruled for 17 years with U.S. support, despite his bloody record.

Democracy was not restored. It was murdered.

Moreover, its killer was **praised for stability**.

The Language of Disguise

Regime change does not begin with bombs. It begins with **language**.

- "Promoting democracy" means backing coups.
- "Restoring order" means dismantling parliaments.
- "Humanitarian intervention" means airstrikes.
- "Supporting civil society" means funding political opposition.
- "Free market reform" means privatizing everything for Western investors.

Moreover, every time it happens, the U.S. government claims it is surprised when the region descends into chaos, as if the fire was not lit from Washington.

Assassinations Without Accountability

Sometimes the coup does not require an army, just a bullet or a drone.

- **Patrice Lumumba**, Congo's first Prime Minister, was assassinated with CIA knowledge in 1961.
- **Qassem Soleimani**, an Iranian general, was killed by a drone strike in 2020, an act widely condemned as illegal under international law.
- **Anwar al-Awlaki**, a U.S. citizen, was executed without trial in Yemen via drone; his teenage son was killed two weeks later.

Each act was justified as "preventing terrorism" or "protecting American lives."

Nevertheless, what legal system do we use to justify extrajudicial killings across sovereign borders?

Moreover, what happens when democracy becomes the excuse for **global execution orders**?

Conclusion: Who Decides What Democracy Looks Like?

When the United States declares a regime illegitimate, the world listens.

However, too often, what makes a regime illegitimate has little to do with justice and everything to do with **defiance**.

- Defiance of U.S. economic interests.
- Defiance of U.S. military alliances.
- Defiance of a global order built in the image of American power.

Moreover, in that defiance, no matter how democratic, lies the justification for destruction.

This is not democracy.

It is **discipline**, with fighter jets and friendly press coverage.

Until we reckon with that truth, we will continue to watch nations rise with hope, only to fall under the weight of a lion that calls itself a liberator.

Works Cited

Kinzer, Stephen. *Overthrow: America's Century of Regime Change from Hawaii to Iraq*. Henry Holt, 2006.

Grandin, Greg. *Empire's Workshop: Latin America, the United States, and the Rise of the New Imperialism*. Metropolitan Books, 2006.

Chomsky, Noam. *Hegemony or Survival*. Metropolitan Books, 2003.

Blum, William. *Killing Hope: U.S. Military and CIA Interventions Since World War II*. Zed Books, 2004.

Ahmed, Nafeez. "How the U.S. Created ISIS." *Middle East Eye*, 2015.

IV. Strategic Alliances with Tyrants

Freedom for Sale to the Highest Bidder

It is a peculiar feature of American diplomacy that it never seems to run out of exceptions.

Democracy, we are told, is non-negotiable. Human rights are universal. Freedom is sacred.

However, if you are sitting on the right resources, control a key trade route, buy enough weapons, or serve as a valuable bulwark against a designated enemy, you are exempt.

You can jail journalists.

You can torture dissidents.

You can criminalize protest, rig elections, and disappear critics.

If you sign the deal, say the right things, and keep a low profile, you will **get a pass**.

This is the quiet transaction at the heart of American foreign policy:

Principles for sale. Freedom, conditional. Loyalty, everything.

The Price of Silence: How Much Does Democracy Cost?

There is no set rate, but the terms are always familiar:

- **Billions of weapons purchases** = silence on human rights.
- **Access to natural resources** = exemption from democratic scrutiny.
- **Support for U.S. military presence** = immunity from criticism.

It is not about how you treat your people.

It is about how you serve Washington's interests.

Let us not pretend otherwise. These are not awkward compromises. They are **strategic alignments**, calculated, funded, and often codified in formal agreements.

Saudi Arabia: The Crown and the Checkbook

There is perhaps no clearer example than Saudi Arabia.

- An absolute monarchy.
- No elections.
- No freedom of the press.
- Systemic gender apartheid.
- Public beheadings, floggings, and brutal suppression of dissent.

However, it remains one of the United States' **closest allies**.

Why?

- It buys **hundreds of billions** in American weapons.
- It controls the world's most critical oil reserves.
- It serves as a counterweight to Iran in U.S. regional strategy.

When journalist Jamal Khashoggi was dismembered inside a Saudi consulate in 2018, in an operation linked directly to Crown Prince Mohammed bin Salman, the world gasped. The U.S. response?

A few sanctions on minor officials.

No pause in arms sales.

No rupture in the "strategic relationship."

As President Trump infamously said:

"They are spending $450 billion... I do not want to lose all that investment."

The price of democracy? Counted in **dollars**, not dignity.

Egypt: The Coup We Chose to Forget

In 2011, the Arab Spring brought hope to Egypt. Protesters overthrew longtime U.S.-backed autocrat Hosni Mubarak. For the first time, the country held democratic elections.

Mohamed Morsi, affiliated with the Muslim Brotherhood, was elected president.

He was ousted in a **military coup** in 2013.

The general who took over, Abdel Fattah el-Sisi, has since presided over:

- Mass arrests of political opponents.
- Torture and death sentences after sham trials.
- The silencing of civil society.

However, Egypt receives over **$1.3 billion in U.S. military aid annually**, second only to Israel.

Why?

- It helps maintain the status quo with Israel.
- It suppresses Islamist movements that the U.S. fears.
- It protects U.S. access to the Suez Canal.

So, the beatings continue. The prisons are filled. Dissidents vanish. And democracy? It becomes a **talking point, not a policy**.

Indonesia: A Massacre Endorsed

In 1965, Indonesia's military, under General Suharto, launched a violent purge of suspected communists. With U.S. intelligence and quiet backing, more than **500,000 people were slaughtered**, peasants, activists, teachers, students.

The U.S. government knew. Declassified documents show it cheered the massacre.

Suharto ruled for over 30 years. He was brutal, corrupt, and loyal to the U.S. economic order.

He opened Indonesia to Western capital, repressed labor unions, and maintained the archipelago's alignment with Washington's Cold War priorities.

The blood was inconvenient. However, the obedience was priceless.

Other "Democratic Exceptions"

- **Rwanda** under Paul Kagame: A model of stability, but deeply authoritarian. No severe U.S. pressure.
- **Jordan** under a hereditary monarchy: Quiet repression overlooked for its alliance with Israel and the U.S.
- **United Arab Emirates**: No elections, but a major buyer of arms and host of U.S. troops.
- **Turkey** under Erdoğan: Jailing journalists and opponents, but a NATO member critical to U.S. strategy.

Each of these regimes violates core tenets of democracy.

Each receives military, economic, or diplomatic cover from the U.S.

The Language of Hypocrisy

To cover this, American leaders use a script filled with euphemisms:

- "Strategic partnership"
- "Stability in the region"
- "Shared interests"
- "Mutual security"
- "Gradual democratic reform"

However, behind those words lies a **brutal clarity**:

Democracy is a means, not an end.

It is applied selectively. It is revoked when it is inconvenient.

Furthermore, it is often discarded altogether in the name of "realpolitik."

Conclusion: The Allies Who Do Not Need to Change

The actual test of U.S. foreign policy is not how it treats its adversaries, but how it treats its friends.

- If democracy were a principle, Saudi Arabia would be sanctioned.
- If human rights were a priority, Egypt would be disarmed.
- If sovereignty mattered, Indonesia's massacre would be remembered, not buried.

Nevertheless, these are not anomalies. They are the foundation of an empire that prefers loyal tyrants over free nations.

The lion still roars about freedom. However, it kneels before oil, markets, and militarized obedience.

Furthermore, until that roar is no longer for sale, democracy will remain a **costume, not a commitment**.

Works Cited

Blum, William. *Killing Hope: U.S. Military and CIA Interventions Since World War II*. Zed Books, 2003.

Chomsky, Noam. *Who Rules the World?* Metropolitan Books, 2016.

Anderson, Jon Lee. "A Tyrant's Allies." *The New Yorker*, 2018.

Jones, Seth G. *America's Strategic Partnerships: Balancing Interests and Values*. RAND Corporation, 2020.

State Department. *U.S. Foreign Military Financing Reports*. U.S. Government, 2015–2023.

Human Rights Watch. *World Reports, 2015–2023*.

Declassified CIA Documents on Indonesia (1965–1966), National Security Archive.

V. Humanitarianism as a Weapon

NGOs, Aid, and the Civil Society Complex

At first glance, there is nothing more noble than humanitarian aid. It speaks the language of compassion. It arrives with food, medicine, education grants, and promises of partnership. It carries logos, not rifles, smiles, not ultimatums. Furthermore, its messengers are often young, bright-eyed, and fluent in the ethics of empathy.

However, behind the banners and bulletproof vests of many U.S.-aligned humanitarian efforts lies a deeper, far more complex reality, one in which **NGOs and aid organizations become extensions of U.S. foreign policy**, not its moral conscience.

This is not an indictment of every development worker, nurse, or peacebuilder.
It is a confrontation with the **structures** they often unknowingly serve, structures that have turned food into leverage, civil society into a surveillance grid, and foreign aid into **the velvet glove of empire**.

Aid as Architecture, Not Altruism

U.S. humanitarian assistance is not apolitical. It is managed by agencies such as:

- The **U.S. Agency for International Development (USAID)**
- The **National Endowment for Democracy (NED)**
- The **International Republican Institute (IRI)** and the **National Democratic Institute (NDI)**
- State Department-aligned think tanks and contractors

These institutions often fund programs with **specific political objectives**, including promoting a pro-Western ideology, countering socialist or nationalist parties, liberalizing markets, and shaping post-conflict constitutions to align with U.S. interests.

An instruction manual aids it.

Not a gift. A **contract**.

Case Study: Venezuela "Democracy" in Disguise

For years, USAID and NED have poured millions into Venezuelan opposition movements, civil society groups, and media networks, openly calling for a "democratic transition." While the Venezuelan government has been authoritarian in key respects, the selective support for opposition actors has crossed the line from encouragement to orchestration.

- In 2019, humanitarian aid was politicized when trucks were sent to Venezuela's border as part of a regime change campaign.
- Opposition leader Juan Guaidó, recognized by the U.S. as "interim president", received direct material and strategic support from Western governments.
- Meanwhile, sanctions imposed by the U.S. crippled the health care system, causing shortages of insulin, cancer treatment, and dialysis equipment.

The people were squeezed between an authoritarian government and a foreign-backed opposition movement.

Furthermore, "humanitarianism" became a **weapon of pressure**, not relief.

Case Study: Haiti, NGOs as Shadow Government

After the devastating 2010 earthquake, billions of dollars in aid flowed into Haiti. However, most of it never reached the Haitian people. International NGOs, U.S. contractors, and administrative overhead absorbed it.

- The Red Cross raised half a billion dollars, yet built only six permanent homes.
- U.S. NGOs received preferential treatment over Haitian organizations.

- USAID contractors bypassed local government structures, effectively **undermining the sovereignty of the host country**.

The result?

- A Haitian state weakened by decades of foreign intervention was further hollowed out.
- The people lost trust in both their government and the foreigners who claimed to help.
- Civil society was fragmented and **reengineered in the image of its funders**.

In Haiti, the disaster wasn't just natural. It was political.

And NGOs became **the de facto rulers**, answerable not to the people, but to donors in Washington.

Case Study: Sudan, Aid and the "Transition" Trap

Following the 2019 ouster of Sudanese dictator Omar al-Bashir, Western governments rushed to support a "democratic transition." Civil society organizations received millions in support, but that support came with ideological filters:

- Groups that aligned with U.S. visions of liberal democracy were prioritized.
- Those with ties to Islamic movements, Pan-Africanist ideologies, or economic sovereignty were marginalized.
- Economic "reforms" included IMF-backed austerity and subsidy cuts, sparking protests among the poor.

Moreover, when the transition faltered and the military retook power in 2021.

The same countries that promised to stand for democracy issued **statements of concern**, but no sanctions.

Moreover, Sudan's democratic movement was left to face tanks **without international cover**.

The NGO-Industrial Complex

Over time, civil society has become **professionalized**, outsourced, and tethered to donor priorities. In many parts of the Global South:

- Activists become "project managers."
- Movements become "deliverables."
- Change is measured in quarterly reports, not justice.
- Entire civic sectors are trained to speak the language of USAID, grant proposals, logframes, and M&E frameworks, while losing touch with grassroots communities.

The very concept of "civil society" is reshaped to serve Western definitions.

And those who reject these models? Branded "uncivil," "radical," or "anti-democratic."

Aid as Counterinsurgency

In conflict zones, aid is increasingly tied to **military strategy**. In Afghanistan, Iraq, and Somalia, humanitarian work was embedded in U.S. counterterrorism efforts:

- Doctors escorted by soldiers.
- Schools are funded only in "cleared" zones.
- Food aid is used to win hearts and minds in contested areas.

This militarization blurred the line between **humanitarianism and occupation**, turning local populations into both foreign soldiers and aid workers.

The message was clear: help only comes if you comply.

Dignity is negotiable. Suffering is strategic.

Conclusion: The Cost of Conditional Compassion

Humanitarian aid should heal.

It should empower.

It should be rooted in solidarity, not supremacy.

However, in the hands of the empire, it becomes something else entirely:

- A tool for soft power.
- A vehicle for influence.
- A leash on democratic experimentation that does not follow U.S. scripts.

Behind the relief tents and grant announcements lie quieter violence:

The erasure of agency. The theft of self-determination. The redesign of resistance.

Until aid is disentangled from control, and until civil society is allowed to breathe without strings, humanitarianism will remain another claw hidden beneath the lion's mane.

Works Cited

Schuller, Mark. *Killing with Kindness: Haiti, International Aid, and NGOs*. Rutgers University Press, 2012.

Chomsky, Noam. *Rogue States: The Rule of Force in World Affairs*. South End Press, 2000.

Berríos, Rubén. "The Politics of Aid and Reconstruction in Haiti." *Journal of Humanitarian Assistance*, 2015.

Prashad, Vijay. *The Poorer Nations: A Possible History of the Global South*. Verso, 2013.

USAID & NED Grant Disclosures (Venezuela, Haiti, Sudan), 2010–2022.

Jean-Baptiste, Rachel. "Who Runs Haiti?" *The Nation*, May 2021.

VI. Proxy Wars Dressed in Principles

Arming Rebels, Toppling Governments, Calling It Freedom

Democracy rarely arrives alone.

In the hands of American foreign policy, it often travels with an entourage of *advisors*, *arms shipments*, and *militias wrapped in press statements about liberty*.

For decades, when the United States did not want to invade directly, or when the optics of war became too costly, it turned to proxy warfare: funding, training, and arming rebel groups to do what it could not openly do itself.

To the world, it is known as this **support for democracy**.

Nevertheless, for the people caught in the crossfire, children in refugee camps, mothers burying sons, civilians watching their homes burn, there was no democracy in sight, only destruction.

Proxy wars do not bring freedom.

They fracture nations, flood them with weapons, and leave scars that last for generations.

The Pattern of Proxy Warfare

The formula has been repeated across continents:

1. Identify a government seen as hostile or "non-aligned."
2. Label its leadership as dictatorial or anti-democratic.
3. Channel funds and weapons to opposition forces, regardless of their ideology or human rights record.
4. Use media to brand these groups as "freedom fighters."
5. Dismiss civilian casualties and instability as the "cost of freedom."

6. Deny responsibility when the rebels turn rogue.

It is a **low-risk, high-control** strategy that often leaves countries in a state of ruin.

However, it is wrapped in the language of uplift, not exploitation.

Case Study: Nicaragua and the Contras

In the 1980s, Nicaragua was governed by the **Sandinistas**, a leftist revolutionary party that overthrew the U.S.-backed Somoza dictatorship. They nationalized resources, expanded healthcare and literacy, and aligned with the Non-Aligned Movement.

To Washington, that was unacceptable.

The U.S. responded by training and arming the **Contras**, a right-wing rebel group notorious for assassinations, village massacres, and drug trafficking.

- Congress banned funding for the Contras.
- The Reagan administration secretly continued support through **the Iran-Contra scandal**.
- Nicaragua was dragged into years of violence, its economy shattered.

The CIA described the Contras as "pro-democracy forces."

Nevertheless, the International Court of Justice ruled the U.S. had **violated international law** by mining Nicaraguan harbors and supporting war crimes.

This was not support for democracy.

It was a vendetta against independence.

Case Study: Syria, Rebels, Regime Change, and Chaos

The Syrian Civil War became a theater for U.S. proxy involvement under the banner of protecting civilians and defeating dictatorship.

- The U.S. trained and armed various Syrian rebel factions, some of which later merged with extremist groups.
- CIA's **"Timber Sycamore"** program funneled weapons that ended up in the hands of jihadists.
- Competing rebel factions turned on each other.
- Civilians were caught in the middle: **500,000+ dead**, millions displaced.

While Bashar al-Assad's regime is undeniably brutal, U.S. intervention did not bring freedom.

It prolonged the war, fragmented the opposition, and allowed groups like ISIS to flourish.

The people asked for bread and dignity.

They received bombs, blockades, and a proxy battlefield.

Case Study: Afghanistan, The Original Blowback

In the 1980s, the U.S. armed and funded the **Mujahideen** to fight the Soviet Union's occupation of Afghanistan.

- Billions in weapons were funneled through Pakistan.
- Fighters from across the Muslim world were recruited and trained.
- After the Soviets withdrew, the country descended into civil war.

Among those U.S.-backed rebels?

Osama bin Laden.

The Mujahideen became the Taliban.

The safe houses became terror camps.

Meanwhile, twenty years later, the U.S. invaded the very nation it helped destabilize, leading to yet another occupation, and another failure dressed as liberation.

Other Examples of U.S. Proxy Support

- **Angola**: U.S. support for UNITA rebels against the MPLA government prolonged the civil war and devastated the nation.
- **Yemen**: U.S. weapons and intelligence to Saudi Arabia indirectly fuel proxy warfare against Houthi rebels, with massive civilian casualties.
- **Ukraine (pre-2014)**: Support for anti-Russian factions through NGOs and security cooperation contributed to the post-Maidan crisis.

Each case was justified by slogans: democracy, stability, and *defense of allies.*

Each left behind broken states, refugee flows, and warlords.

The Human Toll

Proxy wars may be politically convenient, but for ordinary people, they are **hell**:

- Markets collapse.
- Schools are closing.
- Healthcare disappears.
- Child soldiers are conscripted.
- Entire generations grow up with trauma and no memory of peace.

However, in Washington, these tragedies are written off as **strategic necessities**.

Conclusion: The Freedom Fighter Myth

The United States has long claimed that by arming rebels, it is supporting "the will of the people."

However, too often, those rebels are accountable not to the people but to **foreign funders**.

Furthermore, when they fall short of their promised goals or turn brutal, the U.S. distances itself, leaving chaos in its wake.

Proxy warfare is not democracy. It is imperial denial.

It is war on the cheap, death by subcontractor.

Moreover, it is time we called it what it is: **covert conquest, dressed in the robes of righteousness**.

Works Cited

Chomsky, Noam. *Hegemony or Survival: America's Quest for Global Dominance*. Metropolitan Books, 2003.

Kinzer, Stephen. *Overthrow: America's Century of Regime Change from Hawaii to Iraq*. Henry Holt, 2006.

Prashad, Vijay. *The Poorer Nations: A Possible History of the Global South*. Verso, 2013.

Weiner, Tim. *Legacy of Ashes: The History of the CIA*. Anchor Books, 2007.

International Court of Justice. *Case Concerning Military and Paramilitary Activities in and Against Nicaragua (Nicaragua v. United States)*, 1986.

Bergen, Peter. *The Rise and Fall of Osama bin Laden*. Simon & Schuster, 2021.

VII. The Legal Cover, International Law as a Shield for Power

Rules for Thee, Exceptions for Me

International law was supposed to be the great equalizer. Forged in the ashes of world wars, built on the bones of colonized nations, and shaped by those who knew the dangers of unchecked power, it was meant to restrain empires and protect the vulnerable.

However, as history progressed, the dream evolved into something else.

What emerged was not a system of justice for all, but a **hierarchy dressed in neutrality**. The rules remained, but the referees took sides. Moreover, the most prominent players rewrote the playbook as they went along.

At the center of this new legal theatre sits the United States: Championing laws when they serve their aims, dismissing them when they do not.

In the age of the American Empire, law has not restrained power. It has been **used to legitimize it**.

The ICC and the Two-Tier Justice System

The **International Criminal Court (ICC)** was created to try individuals for genocide, war crimes, and crimes against humanity. It promised to hold leaders accountable, regardless of nationality.

However, there is a catch.

- The **U.S. has never ratified the Rome Statute**, which established the ICC.
- When ICC prosecutors attempted to investigate **U.S. actions in Afghanistan**, the Trump administration responded by **sanctioning the ICC's staff**.
- President Biden lifted those sanctions but maintained that **U.S. personnel remain outside ICC jurisdiction**.

Meanwhile, the court has overwhelmingly pursued **African leaders**:

- Sudan's Omar al-Bashir.
- Kenya's Uhuru Kenyatta.
- Libya's Muammar Gaddafi (posthumously).
- Central African Republic, Congo, Uganda , all saw indictments.

The court is not illegitimate. However, it is selectively empowered.

Furthermore, the U.S. has helped design that imbalance, cheering it on when it targets rivals, dismissing it when it knocks on its door.

When Law Becomes a Weapon

International law is invoked when it is useful, and ignored when it is not:

- **Russia's invasion of Ukraine**: condemned (rightly) as a violation of sovereignty.
- **U.S. invasion of Iraq**: no Security Council resolution, no accountability.
- **Israeli annexations and military operations**: condemned by the UN but consistently vetoed by the U.S. at the Security Council.
- **Cuba embargo**: condemned annually by the UN General Assembly, yet the U.S. persists, defying the consensus.

Furthermore, when the International Court of Justice (ICJ) ruled in 1986 that the U.S. had violated international law by supporting the Contras in Nicaragua and mining its harbors?

The U.S. **ignored the ruling** and withdrew its recognition of the ICJ's jurisdiction.

Law, it seems, is optional when you are the enforcer.

The "Rules-Based Order", Whose Rules?

U.S. leaders often invoke the phrase *"rules-based international order"*. It sounds noble. However, ask leaders in the Global South, and you will hear another story:

- Rules designed in **Bretton Woods**, without African or Asian voices.
- Trade laws that protect patents but not indigenous land.

- IMF conditionalities that force deregulation but ignore labor rights.
- Sanctions regimes that cripple entire nations while exempting allies.

The "order" in question often means:

U.S.-led institutions enforcing U.S.-favored rules for U.S.-defined ends.

Case Study: Israel and the Shield of U.S. Veto Power

Since 1972, the U.S. has used its **UN Security Council veto over 40 times** to block resolutions critical of Israel, including:

- Condemnations of illegal settlements.
- Calls to halt military operations in Gaza.
- Demands for investigations into civilian deaths.

This consistent shield has not only protected Israeli impunity, but it has **undermined the legitimacy** of international law for millions who witness the suffering but see no accountability.

Meanwhile, Palestinian appeals to the ICC and ICJ are often stalled or denounced as "politically motivated."

It is not that the law does not exist.

Its **enforcement depends on your friends**.

Case Study: The "War on Terror" and Legal Stretching

After 9/11, the U.S. declared a global "war on terror", with no geographic or temporal limit. Under the 2001 Authorization for Use of Military Force (AUMF), it launched operations in:

- Afghanistan
- Iraq
- Somalia

- Yemen
- Pakistan
- Libya
- Syria

Drone strikes, renditions, black sites, indefinite detention, all justified under a broad legal umbrella that the international community never formally endorsed.

Guantanamo Bay remains open.

CIA torture architects remain unchanged.

International law, again, becomes a tool of **rhetoric, not restraint**.

Conclusion: The Law of the Powerful

International law still matters. However, its credibility hinges on consistency.

When laws apply only to the weak, the disobedient, or the non-aligned, they cease to be law and become **levers of empire**.

The lion roars about legal norms. Nevertheless, behind closed doors, it writes exemptions for itself and its allies.

Furthermore, in that double standard, democracy becomes a disguise.

Not a doctrine of freedom, but a performance of legitimacy.

A legal theater, choreographed to shield conquest.

Works Cited

Falk, Richard. *Power Shift: On the New Global Order*. Zed Books, 2016.

Blum, William. *Rogue State: A Guide to the World's Only Superpower*. Zed Books, 2005.

International Criminal Court. *Cases and Jurisdiction Reports*, 2002–2023.

United Nations General Assembly. *Voting Records on U.S. Embargoes and Vetoes*, 1972–2023.

International Court of Justice. *Nicaragua v. United States*, 1986 Judgment.

Ratner, Michael. *The Trial of Donald Rumsfeld: A Prosecution by Book*. New Press, 2008.

Reprieve & Amnesty International. *Drone Warfare and International Law*, 2015.

VIII. The Global Architecture of Empire

Bases, Sanctions, and Surveillance

You cannot see it on most maps.

You will not find it in campaign speeches.

However, spread across every ocean and nestled into every continent lies the quiet muscle of the American empire: **a web of military bases, economic chokepoints, and digital eyes** trained on the world.

This is not an empire as spectacle. It is an empire as infrastructure.

Built over decades. Maintained through budgets, treaties, and silence.

It does not roar. It **hovers, watches, and waits**, ready to reward compliance or punish disobedience.

Furthermore, all of its bases, the sanctions, and the surveillance operate beneath the guise **of democracy**.

The Base Empire: 750 Outposts of "Security"

The United States operates **more than 750 military bases** in at least 80 countries, **more than any other nation or empire in history**. These outposts are not temporary. They are concrete, fenced, fortified facts:

- Ramstein Air Base in Germany: critical for U.S. drone operations.
- Camp Lemonnier in Djibouti: a launchpad into the Horn of Africa.
- Al Udeid in Qatar: housing thousands of troops and advanced surveillance technology.
- Okinawa in Japan: a permanent presence since WWII.
- Diego Garcia: a remote island converted into a secretive logistical hub.

These installations house drones, bombers, special forces, nuclear assets, and command centers. And their stated purpose? **Security, deterrence, humanitarian assistance**.

However, for the local populations who live beside them, the experience is often one of:

- Land seizures
- Sexual violence and environmental damage
- Political interference
- Suppressed sovereignty

These are not embassies. They are **anchors of enforcement**.

Sanctions: Economic Warfare by Another Name

When bombs are not dropped, **sanctions are deployed**. And make no mistake, they kill too.

Sanctions, often justified as "tools of diplomacy," are economic **sieges**. They restrict trade, isolate economies, collapse currencies, and starve governments of the resources needed to function.

Who suffers?

- **Children in Iran** are denied access to cancer drugs.

- **The elderly in Venezuela are** unable to afford food under hyperinflation.
- **Hospitals in North Korea** are short on essential supplies.

These are not surgical measures. They are **blanket punishments**, imposed not by international consensus, but by U.S. policy.

Over 40 countries are currently under U.S. sanctions.

However, America calls itself the defender of "free markets."

Case Study: Venezuela, Choking an Economy

After Hugo Chávez's government nationalized oil and pursued socialist policies, the U.S. began a slow campaign of economic strangulation:

- Banking restrictions blocked international payments.
- Oil trade was crippled.
- U.S. allies were pressured not to engage.

Under Nicolás Maduro, these sanctions escalated, contributing to **a humanitarian crisis** that saw mass emigration, medicine shortages, and fuel lines stretching for miles.

The stated aim? "Restoring democracy."

The result? Economic collapse and the **collective punishment** of 30 million people.

Case Study: Iran, Permanent Siege

Since 1979, Iran has lived under the shadow of U.S. sanctions. Following the 2015 nuclear deal, there was brief relief, until the Trump administration withdrew in 2018 and **reimposed a "maximum pressure" campaign**.

- Oil exports plummeted.
- Currency values fell.

- Covid-19 relief supplies were blocked.

The Iranian government remained defiant. However, ordinary shopkeepers, nurses, and students paid the price.

Sanctions did not spark reform. They deepened resentment. Moreover, democracy does not grow in a strangled garden.

Digital Domination: Surveillance Without Borders

The global reach of American surveillance is not fiction. It is a fact, confirmed by whistleblowers like **Edward Snowden** and exposed through programs like **PRISM**, **XKeyscore**, and **ECHELON**.

- U.S. agencies monitor foreign governments, corporations, journalists, and civilians.
- Allies like **Germany, France, and Brazil** have been caught in the dragnet.
- Leaders like **Angela Merkel and Dilma Rousseff** had their phones tapped.

All justified in the name of **national security**.

None is subject to international oversight.

In the digital age, democracy does not require thanks.

It just requires **data** and the power to weaponize it.

The Myth of Benevolence

Through bases, sanctions, and surveillance, the U.S. projects power far beyond its shores. However, its public image remains one of restraint, of reluctant leadership, of principled engagement.

Nevertheless, look closer, and you will see:

- **The base in your backyard may be tracking your neighbors.**
- **The aid package may be tied to a vote at the UN.**

- **The satellite overhead may be watching a protest.**

Democracy is what the lion claims to bring.

However, its claws are **embedded in the world's supply chains, hard drives, and border controls**.

Conclusion: The Empire Beneath the Flag

The empire that America claims not to be is very alive.

It does not build pyramids or carve statues. It builds systems, visible and invisible, that make resistance difficult and **compliance profitable**.

Its currency is the dollar.

Its infrastructure is global.

Its defense is **plausible deniability**.

Until we acknowledge this architecture, not as an accident, but as an intentional design, there can be no honest reckoning with democracy.

Because the lion does not just roar.

It **surrounds**, **surveils**, and **suffocates**, then offers to help you breathe.

Works Cited

Blum, William. *Rogue State: A Guide to the World's Only Superpower*. Zed Books, 2005.

Gordon, Joy. *Invisible War: The United States and the Iraq Sanctions*. Harvard University Press, 2010.

Snowden, Edward. *Permanent Record*. Metropolitan Books, 2019.

Prashad, Vijay. *Washington Bullets: A History of the CIA, Coups, and Assassinations*. LeftWord Books, 2020.

UN Human Rights Council. *Impact of Unilateral Coercive Measures*, 2021.

Shah, Anup. "The U.S. Military's Global Footprint." *Global Issues*, 2023.

American Civil Liberties Union. *Surveillance in the Digital Age*, 2022.

IX. Conclusion: The Lion's Mane Is Not Freedom, It Is Camouflage

When the Cloak Slips, So Does the Illusion

There is a haunting honesty to an old empire when it no longer hides what it is. Rome never claimed to liberate Gaul. The British did not pretend to bring democracy to Bengal. They ruled with flags, fleets, and fortresses, and they made no apologies.

However, America was different.
Its empire arrived dressed in rhetoric.
It spoke not of domination, but of **liberty**.

It landed on foreign shores not with coronation, but with **campaign slogans**.

"We are here to help."
"We are building democracy."
"We are protecting your future."

Moreover, for a time, many believed it may be because they wanted to. Maybe because the alternatives, totalitarianism, civil war, and famine, seemed worse. Alternatively, maybe because the lion was so well-dressed, so rehearsed, so righteous, that it was hard to believe the blood on its paws.

Nevertheless, now, the disguise is fraying.

A Global Reckoning

Across continents, the illusion is cracking:

- In **Iraq**, democracy came in the form of tanks and torture chambers.
- In **Haiti**, it came with assassinated presidents and unaccountable NGOs.

- In **Libya**, it brought open-air slave markets, and a nation ripped to shreds.
- In **Palestine**, it arrived with tear gas, walls, and silence.
- In **Africa**, it wore a diplomatic suit, but whispered IMF terms behind every handshake.

Furthermore, all the while, the U.S. called itself a "force for good."

However, the good was always conditional.

The freedom was always prepackaged.

The self-determination was always negotiated **under watchful eyes**.

The lion, it turns out, was not leading. It was **patrolling**.

The Cost of the Performance

The real cost of America's democracy theater is not just measured in bombs dropped or coups funded. It is measured in **hope betrayed**:

- In the young Syrian who marched for bread and dignity, only to be caught between Assad's barrel bombs and U.S.-armed rebels.
- In the Congolese mother whose land was sold by her government to an American mining firm in the name of "development."
- In the Afghan teacher who welcomed the end of the Taliban, only to see her school destroyed by a drone strike "accident."
- In the Haitian child born beneath an NGO flag, whose country remains occupied not by troops, but by consultants with clipboards and contracts.

These are not failures. They are **designs**.

They are how democracy has been exported, leveraged, and manipulated, not to free, but to control.

Reclaiming Meaning from the Mask

Democracy, in its most valid form, is sacred.

- It is people who decide their fate.
- It is power accountable to the many, not the few.
- It is the freedom to speak, to dissent, to dream, , on one's terms.

However, when democracy becomes a brand, when it becomes a weapon, when it is used to justify torture, surveillance, sanctions, and subversion, it loses its soul.

Moreover, when that soul is gone, the lion's mane is no longer a crown of legitimacy.

It is **camouflage**, hiding fangs beneath fine phrases.

The Final Truth

America does not need to abandon democracy.

However, it must stop using democracy as **a cover** for greed, for war, for empire.

The lion must look in the mirror.

Not to roar more loudly, but to ask a more complex question:

Who have we become beneath the mane?

Until that question is answered, the world will continue to resist, not America's people, not its ideals, but its **mask**.

Because behind every bomb labeled "freedom," there is a memory. Behind every sanction called "justice," there is a grave. And behind every regime toppled for the sake of "democratic values," there is a community left to bury its dead, and build again from the rubble.

Works Cited

Blum, William. *Killing Hope: U.S. Military and CIA Interventions Since World War II.* Zed Books, 2003.

Chomsky, Noam. *Hegemony or Survival: America's Quest for Global Dominance*. Metropolitan Books, 2003.

Grandin, Greg. *Empire's Workshop: Latin America, the United States, and the Rise of the New Imperialism*. Metropolitan Books, 2006.

Prashad, Vijay. *The Darker Nations: A People's History of the Third World*. The New Press, 2008.

Mamdani, Mahmood. *Saviors and Survivors: Darfur, Politics, and the War on Terror*. Pantheon Books, 2009.

Human Rights Watch. *World Report 2023: Events of 2022*. HRW, 2023.

UN Office for the Coordination of Humanitarian Affairs. *Global Humanitarian Overview*, 2022.

Chapter 4 Recap: Beneath the Mane, Democracy as a Cover for Empire

The Language of Liberty, the Machinery of Domination

Chapter 4 peels back the lion's mane, the well-rehearsed image of the United States as the global guardian of democracy, to reveal the brutal architecture hidden underneath. What we find is not liberty, it is leverage. Not uplift, but **control**. This chapter exposes how democracy has been weaponized, instrumentalized, and commodified in the service of U.S. empire-building.

It opens by framing the contradiction: the same country that claims to defend democracy often undermines it through **military interventions**, **support for autocrats**, and **economic warfare**. Democracy, it argues, has become a **costume for conquest**, a rhetorical device to justify regime change, coups, sanctions, and surveillance.

Key Themes and Findings:

1. Democracy's Double Mask

The U.S. acts as both preacher and enforcer, using noble language publicly, while deploying force and coercion privately. Duality allows it to **preach values while violating them**, and to punish disobedient states under the guise of protecting freedom.

2. Regime Change as "Democratic Intervention"

From **Iraq** to **Libya** to **Chile**, the chapter details how the U.S. has used military invasions and CIA-backed coups to remove elected or non-compliant governments. These operations are always branded as "liberation," yet they leave behind chaos, civil war, and broken sovereignty.

3. Strategic Partnerships with Tyrants

Alliances with **Saudi Arabia, Egypt, Israel**, and others expose the hypocrisy of U.S. democracy promotion. If a regime serves U.S. interests, militarily, economically, or geopolitically, it gets a pass, no matter how repressive. **Loyalty trumps liberty**.

4. The NGO and Aid Industrial Complex

Humanitarianism and the funding of civil society have become soft tools of intervention. Aid, NGOs, and training programs often work not to empower, but to **re-engineer political systems** to reflect U.S. preferences, particularly in **Haiti**, **Venezuela**, and **Sudan**.

5. Proxy Warfare

When direct military intervention is too costly, the U.S. turns to proxy wars, arming rebels in **Syria**, **Afghanistan**, **Nicaragua**, and elsewhere. Branded as "freedom fighters," these groups often unleash devastation, radicalism, and long-term instability.

6. International Law as a Selective Weapon

International norms are enforced only when convenient. The U.S. ignores **ICJ and ICC** rulings when they implicate its own actions but insists on legal accountability for its rivals. This selective enforcement undermines the legitimacy of international law itself.

7. The Global Architecture of Empire

The U.S. controls the globe not just through narrative, but through physical and digital infrastructure:

- **750+ military bases**
- **Sweeping sanctions regimes**
- **Global surveillance networks**

Together, these systems form a hidden empire, exerting pressure, gathering data, and enforcing obedience under the guise of protection.

Final Reflection:

The chapter closes with a sobering truth: the United States does not export democracy. It **rents it out**, with conditions. It sells it to the highest bidder. Furthermore, when a nation resists the terms of that sale, the lion does not roar with **impunity**.

The mane is not made of freedom. It is **camouflage**, hiding the teeth of economic warfare, military force, and political manipulation.

Until we reckon with how democracy has been used not as a gift, but as a leash, we will keep mistaking empire for justice, and **occupation for order**.

Chapter 5:

Puppets and Parliaments, Democracy Without Sovereignty

Staged Elections, Imported Constitutions, and the Illusion of Choice

Chapter Theme

This chapter pulls back the velvet curtain on a global performance, where elections are held, constitutions are adopted, parliaments are opened, and leaders are sworn in with a grand ceremony and applause. To the untrained eye, it appears to be a democracy. The flags wave, the press corps watches. Foreign observers nod.

The power? It is somewhere else.

Somewhere in a European capital, a boardroom in New York, or a military base outside the capital city. Somewhere offstage, decisions are made that no ballot can touch. Furthermore, that is the heart of this chapter: **democracy without sovereignty is an illusion**. A theater in which the cast performs, but the script is written by others.

Across Africa, Latin America, the Middle East, and Asia, too many nations have been handed the *form* of democracy, while being denied the *function*. Constitutions drafted by foreign lawyers. Economies regulated by the IMF. Embassies vetted political candidates. Civil society is funded more by USAID than by grassroots communities.

It is not that people don't vote.It's that their votes do not impact what truly matters. It is not that governments are not elected. It is that governance is still outsourced.

What does it mean to elect a parliament that cannot reject a loan? What is the meaning of a constitution if it cannot defend land from privatization?

What dignity is there in democracy if sovereignty is signed away?

This chapter examines the structure of that contradiction, the way foreign-supported democracies imitate freedom while tying nations to policies they didn't create. It shows how liberation is redefined as technical help, how opposition is controlled through grants, and how leaders are promoted for loyalty rather than legitimacy.

And most importantly, it honors those who have seen through the show.
Those who demand real power, not just performance. Those who understand that a parliament without sovereignty isn't a temple of the people; it is a stage with puppets instead of leaders.

This is the story of parliaments without power. Of elections without agency. Of democracy, **unrooted, rented, and restrained.**

And the increasing refusal to play the part.

I. The Spectacle of Self-Governance

When Democracy Becomes Performance Without Power

There's a hush that settles over the room when a nation votes for the first time after war or dictatorship. Flags flutter, international monitors take photos, and CNN films polling lines. The new president shows their inked thumb or a copy of the newly approved constitution. Headlines read: "Democracy at Last."

What the world doesn't see is who edited that constitution.

Who approved the candidates?

Who guaranteed the loans that will shape every budget for the next thirty years?

Who left just before the cameras arrived?

This is the spectacle of self-governance, an act performed for legitimacy but scripted from abroad. It is the modern masquerade of democracy in the Global South: celebrated worldwide, but empty at its core.

The Form, Not the Freedom

We live in a world where the outward appearance of democracy matters more than its actual substance.

- Do you hold elections? Check.
- Do you have a multi-party system? Check.
- Did you ratify a constitution with "rights" written in it? Check.

Now you qualify for trade deals, aid packages, and glowing press from Western media.

However, underneath the surface, the conditions for genuine self-rule are **absent**:

- **Land reform? Blocked by foreign investors.**
- **Currency devaluation? Demanded by the IMF.**
- **Energy subsidies? Slashed to meet loan targets.**
- **Military independence? Trained, funded, and surveilled by U.S. operatives.**

It's like being handed the keys to a house, but only allowed to live in one room. With someone else holding the deed.

Constitutions as Contracts, Not Covenants

Many nations emerging from conflict or colonialism are praised for adopting democratic constitutions. However, who wrote those documents?

Often, the fine print of a "people's constitution" is drafted in conference centers thousands of miles away. Teams of Western legal experts arrive with templates in hand, boilerplate provisions on decentralization, property rights, and anti-corruption enforcement. On paper, these are neutral. In practice, they often deepen neoliberal economics, privatize public goods, and centralize power in technocratic institutions that cater to global markets rather than citizens.

And the people? They are asked to vote on a document most of them have not read, written in legalese, and with no ability to amend it meaningfully.

It is not that these constitutions are entirely bad; it is that they are **pre-approved blueprints**, designed to serve creditors before communities.

Who Governs?

Ask yourself: What defines a government?

- Are elections held every four years?
- Or is it being able to say *no* to a foreign military base?
- Is it the symbolism of a president in a suit?
- Or is it the power to renegotiate debt, protect resources, or reject conditions that harm your people?

In many U.S.-supported "democracies," the elected officials cannot touch the most vital decisions. The central bank answers foreign lenders, the military answers to Western trainers. The health system is built around donor benchmarks. The economy is tied to the dollar.

You can run the country, but only if you run it *their* way.

The Optics of Inclusion, The Reality of Control

There is a cruel irony in how carefully the stage is managed:

- Gender parity in parliament? Yes.
- Diversity in cabinet posts? Yes.
- Can those officials redirect aid, protect local industries, or defy Western interests?

Rarely.

In this model, representation is granted, but **redistribution is forbidden**. Political inclusion becomes a kind of **window dressing**, a soft power showcase meant to prove democracy is thriving, while the strings of sovereignty are pulled from offstage.

And how can we resist this model? How do we ask for a different path?

That's when the words shift. Suddenly, you're labeled as "radical," "populist," "illiberal," or "threatening to stability."

Democracy as Theater, Sovereignty as Prop

To the world, it all looks clean and orderly:

- A parliament in session.
- A constitution held aloft.
- Civil society representatives nodding in roundtables.
- Aid flowing from embassies.
- Monitors releasing glowing reports.

However, real governance takes place elsewhere, in Washington, Brussels, at the IMF headquarters, and during meetings with defense attachés.

This is democracy as a managed spectacle. It presents a paradox: the more "democratic" a country seems to Western audiences, the less sovereign it might truly be.

Democracy becomes the stage. Sovereignty? That is still **behind the curtain**.

Conclusion: The Performance Ends at the Border

This section ends with a provocation: What happens when the audience stops clapping?

What occurs when people realize they are not actors, but props? When are they showcased to the world as proof of democratic progress while being left out of actual decisions?

That's when the play starts to fall apart.

That's when movements begin to rise.

That's when leaders emerge and declare, “We want more than applause. We want power.”

Moreover, that is when the lion, still cloaked in democracy, **begins to growl**.

II. The Illusion of Choice, Elections in a Cage

When You Can Vote for Anything but Your Freedom

Every four or five years, a flag is raised, a campaign is launched, and a nation heads to the polls. Observers arrive. Ballots are cast. Fingers are dipped in ink. Victory speeches echo through the parliament buildings, newly painted for the cameras.

The world observes and agrees: “This is progress.”

What about the people? Many are aware of the truth.

They vote. And little changes. Their water is still privatized. Their wages are still suppressed. Their leaders, no matter how “new,” still answer to the same embassies, the same loan officers, the same foreign investors.

It’s not that they can’t choose. It’s what they’re allowed to choose that has already been decided.

This is democracy in a cage: elections without agency, ballots within borders drawn by power, and governance that ends where foreign interests begin.

Pre-Approved Opposition: The Vote You’re Authorized to Cast

In many so-called democratic transitions supported by the United States or its allies, candidates who challenge the status quo, the economic system, military alliances, or the influence of Western corporations are marginalized, jailed, or delegitimized.

The ballot only shows diversity in names.

- Different faces, same foreign-aligned platforms.
- Multiple parties all agree with the IMF terms.
- Debates over everything, except sovereignty.

This is not pluralism. It is **political choreography**, with dissent carefully managed, and the range of policy options **narrowed by design**.

In the words of political theorist Sheldon Wolin, what emerges is "managed democracy", a system where participation is permitted, but outcomes are predetermined (Wolin, Democracy Incorporated, 2008).

Case Study: Afghanistan (2004–2021), Voting Under Occupation

After the U.S.-led invasion of Afghanistan, the country was quickly reorganized into a "democratic republic." Elections were conducted. Western media heralded women's voting and the sight of purple-stained fingers raised high.

Beneath the surface, power stayed with the occupying forces and their allies.

- **U.S. officials vetted presidential candidates**.
- Warlords with U.S. support retained vast regional control.
- Corruption increased as foreign aid was used for political patronage.
- The Taliban's resurgence was fueled not just by ideology, but by the **widespread recognition that the government had no independence**.

In 2021, when the U.S. withdrew, the Afghan government collapsed in a matter of days. No mass resistance. No national defense. No illusion left.

It was not a democracy. It was a **client regime wrapped in ballots**.

(Rashid, *Descent into Chaos*, 2021; Ahmed, "How the War Was Lost," *The Nation*, 2021)

When Elections Reinforce Dependence

In many nations across the Global South, elections are held regularly, but Economic and security policies are outsourced:

- Loan agreements specify budget terms.
- Trade policy is embedded in Western-drafted bilateral deals.
- Education reforms are designed to satisfy donors.
- Foreign troops, often uninvited by the public, are stationed indefinitely.

In such contexts, elections serve as tools of validation, not change. They signal to the world, "All is well," even as the people know they are stuck in contracts they did not vote for.

Voting is no longer about who governs, it is about who gets to wear the mask of governance.

"Free and Fair", But for Whom?

The phrase "free and fair elections" has become the highest standard of Legitimacy. Who sets that standard?

- An election may be free, but what if key candidates are imprisoned or exiled?
- It may be fair, but what if Western-funded NGOs dominate public messaging?
- It may be peaceful, but what if the most critical policies are off-limits to change?

Elections are judged "successful" when they meet procedural benchmarks, not when they result in **empowered people or accountable states**.

As Cameroonian philosopher Achille Mbembe puts it, *"Post colony elections are often rituals of loyalty, not exercises of will."* (Mbembe, *On the Post colony*, 2001)

The Cost of Illusion

The damage caused by hollow elections is not only symbolic; it is emotional and psychological. It fosters despair, cynicism, and eventually, rage.

- Youth who vote may see no job opportunities.
- Farmers who vote might lose land to multinational agribusiness.
- Women who vote could watch foreign-backed militaries support abusers.

Over time, trust erodes, not just in leaders but also in the very concept of self-rule. In that vacuum, extremism flourishes, not because people hate democracy, but because its shadow has **betrayed them**.

Conclusion: The Ballot Without the Backbone

Voting matters. Participation matters. Not when the outcome is **cosmetic**. Not when the state is a stage and the script is written abroad.

This is the illusion we must confront: that democracy begins and ends with elections. It doesn't. Democracy starts with **sovereignty**. It begins when a nation can say "no" to foreign pressure, "yes" to its priorities, and "enough" to the pretense of choice.

Until then, elections remain beautiful, colorful, widely televised, but hollow. A ballot in a cage.

Works Cited

Wolin, Sheldon. *Democracy Incorporated: Managed Democracy and the Specter of Inverted Totalitarianism*. Princeton University Press, 2008.

Mbembe, Achille. *On the Postcolony*. University of California Press, 2001.

Rashid, Ahmed. *Descent Into Chaos: The United States and the Failure of Nation Building in Pakistan, Afghanistan, and Central Asia*. Viking, 2021.

Ahmed, Azmat. "How the War Was Lost." *The Nation*, August 2021.

Kaldor, Mary. *New and Old Wars: Organized Violence in a Global Era*. Stanford University Press, 2012.

III. Constitutions from the Outside, Governance by Ghostwriters

When the Founding Document Is Not Yours to Write

Every nation deserves a birth story, one that springs from the sweat of its people, shaped by its struggle, written in its voice. For most, that story is a constitution: the document that defines who they are, what they value, and how they choose to govern themselves.

In much of the post-colonial world, that story has been written behind the scenes.

Drafted not in community halls or liberation assemblies, but in international conference rooms. Reviewed not by local elders or national thinkers, but by legal consultants flown in from Washington, London, or Brussels. Edited to meet the standards of foreign investors and donors, not the needs of the people who must live under it.

This is governance by ghostwriters, a subtle yet powerful form of imperial control. Not through bullets. Not through occupation. Through clauses, chapters, and conditionalities.

The Foreign Pen in the National Charter

Foreign involvement in constitution-making is often justified as "technical support." It amounts to political steering, embedding Western legal and economic priorities into the core of a new or transitioning state.

- Independent central banks that answer international lenders rather than parliaments.

- Private property protections are designed to reassure multinational corporations.
- Decentralization mandates that weaken national governments while empowering local elites aligned with donor interests.
- Anti-corruption courts supervised by foreign consultants or shaped to mirror Western models.

These are not just legal tools. They are **mechanisms of control**.

And when codified into the highest law of the land, they become unbreakable chains, disguised as democratic norms.

Case Study: Iraq (2005), A Constitution Under Occupation

After the U.S. invasion in 2003, Iraq was pressured to adopt a new constitution quickly, less than two years after the fall of Saddam Hussein.

- The drafting committee operated under **U.S. occupation**, with American officials overseeing every step.
- Key provisions, such as oil revenue sharing and federalism, were included to **ensure decentralized control over natural resources**, aligning with Western and corporate interests (Anderson & Stansfield, *The Future of Iraq*, 2005).
- Many Iraqis **did not understand or trust** the document they were asked to vote on in the 2005 referendum.

What emerged was not a unifying charter. It was a **compromise document**, designed to appease outside powers and divide internal opposition.

Iraq was given a constitution. It wasn't really one it could call its own.

Case Study: Kenya (2010), Reform in the Shadow of Foreign Pressure

Kenya's 2010 constitutional referendum was praised as a major milestone in its democratic growth. The new constitution expanded rights, reorganized power, and added checks and balances. Behind the praise, many Kenyans questioned who had the loudest voice in the process.

- International donors, especially the U.S. and the UK, funded and influenced the civic education campaigns.
- Key reforms mirrored donor priorities: judicial independence, land reforms, and anti-terror legislation aligned with the "war on terror."
- Some sections were **rushed or unclear**, and subsequent implementation was shaped by external benchmarks rather than community consensus.

While the constitution had positive aspects, it also reflected **foreign fingerprints**, raising the question: *Whose democracy was it?*

Constitution as Contract, Not Covenant

When constitutions are created to comfort foreign donors, they start to look like **contracts, not covenants**.

- Contracts protect the investor.
- Covenants protect the people.

And when clauses are embedded that call for fiscal austerity, restrict public land ownership, or enforce "good governance" as defined by outsiders, the constitution becomes a **legal straitjacket**, not a foundation for national freedom.

The people are told, "This is your highest law." They were not permitted to write it genuinely.

Legal Colonialism: The New Empire of Advisors

This phenomenon has a name: **legal colonialism**.

- Former colonies were handed post-independence constitutions modeled after their colonizers.

- In the 21st century, they are handed "reforms" shaped by **legal consultants**, **multilateral agencies**, and **NGO-funded think tanks**.
- These actors often lack real ties to the communities they serve, and are only answerable to donor budgets and diplomatic missions.

Their presence is rarely questioned because their language is benevolent. They speak of "good governance," "rule of law," and "inclusive politics."

Their impact can be destabilizing, deepening neoliberal reforms, empowering technocrats over traditional leaders, and transforming political culture into ways that feel unfamiliar and imposed.

Conclusion: A Constitution Is Only Democratic If It Is Yours

A constitution should not just protect sovereignty. It should **express it**.

It should carry the weight of local voices, histories, languages, and values.

It should be debated in marketplaces, in churches and mosques, in schools and neighborhoods, not just in five-star hotels and donor-funded workshops.

Until people have the power to shape their future, democracy remains superficial.

Moreover, when the founding document is ghostwritten, the nation becomes a shadow of its freedom.

Works Cited

Anderson, Liam, and Gareth Stansfield. *The Future of Iraq: Dictatorship, Democracy, or Division?* Palgrave Macmillan, 2005.

Chimni, B. S. "The Past, Present and Future of International Law: A Critical Third World Approach." *Melbourne Journal of International Law*, vol. 8, 2007.

Mbaye, Sanou. "Neocolonial Constitutionalism." *Pambazuka News*, 2010.

Cheeseman, Nic. *How to Rig an Election*. Yale University Press, 2018.

Kapur, Devesh, and Richard Webb. *Beyond the IMF: The Post-Adjustment Era in Africa and Latin America*. Zed Books, 2000.

Gathii, James T. "The Use and Abuse of African Constitutions." *Harvard International Law Journal*, vol. 56, 2015.

IV. Parliaments Without Power, Governments in Debt Chains

When Democracy Cannot Say "No"

To the outside world, parliaments are symbols of national power. Inside those chambers, men and women stand behind polished podiums, reading bills, debating budgets, and casting votes under national flags. Camera flash. Applause breaks out. Constitutions are quoted.

However, in too many areas of the world, that image is just that, an image.

Behind the curtains and under the floorboards lie the terms of surrender signed decades ago. Loan agreements. Memoranda of understanding. Conditionality packages. Furthermore, they whisper louder than the speakers at the podium.

These governments may be elected. However, they are not free.

They cannot raise the minimum wage without triggering concerns about inflation from the IMF. They cannot subsidize food without violating fiscal targets. They cannot protect local industries without being accused of protectionism by the WTO. They cannot default, restructure, or even negotiate without consequences.

This is **a democracy chained by debt**. Moreover, no matter how many parties compete or how many voters turn out, the decisions that matter, about food, fuel, wages, and water, are already made.

Debt as a Weapon of Soft Conquest

Debt is not just a financial tool. It is a **geopolitical instrument**.

In the post-colonial era, as former colonies began charting their paths, many fell into debt traps, some inherited from colonial administrations, others created through aggressive development loans pushed by Western banks and multilateral institutions.

By the 1980s and 1990s, as debt ballooned, institutions such as the International Monetary Fund (IMF) and the **World Bank** stepped in, not just to lend, but to **reshape entire economies**.

Their prescription?

- Privatize state assets.
- Cut public sector wages.
- Eliminate subsidies.
- Peg currency values.
- Remove trade protections.

These reforms were marketed as "stabilization." In reality, they were **structural realignments** that transferred control of national economies to outside forces.

Once the chains were on, they became difficult to break.

Case Study: Ghana, A Model Pupil with Tied Hands

Ghana is often praised as a democratic success story in Africa. It has held multiple peaceful elections, experienced transfers of power, and built robust civil institutions.

Meanwhile, beneath its electoral maturity lies economic vulnerability.

Since the 1980s, Ghana has signed numerous structural adjustment agreements with the IMF and World Bank. These deals were imposed:

- Massive cuts to public services.
- Reductions in agricultural subsidies.
- Free trade policies that exposed local industries to foreign competition.

Even as new governments were elected, their room to maneuver was narrow. They inherited debt and conditionalities they could not defy without risking currency collapse, aid suspension, or capital flight.

In 2022, facing inflation and soaring public debt, Ghana once again approached the IMF, its 17th time since independence.

The parliament remained intact. However, its power was bound by the invisible contracts of creditors.

(Mkandawire, 2005; Stiglitz, *Globalization and Its Discontents*, 2002)

When Budgets Serve Banks, Not People

The most sacred act of governance is the budget. It reflects the values of a nation, what people get, and why.

However, in debt-bound democracies, budgets are often reviewed by foreign institutions before being presented to local parliaments. Loan agreements require governments to:

- Limit wage increases for civil servants.
- Cut subsidies for fuel, food, or electricity.
- Increase regressive taxes (such as VAT) that disproportionately affect the poor.
- Open public services to private investors, often from the Global North.

The result?

- **Governments become bill collectors**, not service providers.
- Parliamentarians can pass symbolic resolutions, but real power lies with economists in Washington, D.C., or Brussels.

Austerity is passed down like scripture. Moreover, those who question it are branded irresponsible.

Case Study: Tunisia, A Revolution Hijacked by Creditors

Following the Arab Spring's toppling of Tunisia's dictatorship in 2011, the country held democratic elections and adopted a new constitution.

Nevertheless, by 2020, Tunisia's democracy was in crisis, **not from authoritarianism, but from economic strangulation**.

- IMF-backed reforms led to subsidy cuts and public wage freezes.
- Unemployment soared. Youth disillusionment deepened.
- Public services crumbled, while debt payments consumed more than 20% of the national budget.

When protests erupted over rising prices and joblessness, Western media asked if Tunisia's democratic experiment was failing.

Nonetheless, the reality was more sobering:

Tunisia had democracy, yes. However, it lacked economic sovereignty to make it a reality.

(Kilani, 2020; IMF Tunisia Country Report, 2021)

The Language of Coercion

These policies are rarely presented as impositions. They're framed as:

- "Recommendations"
- "Best practices"
- "Good governance reforms"
- "Benchmarks for disbursement"

However, refusal comes with consequences:

- Credit downgrades.
- Frozen aid.

- Trade penalties.
- Investor flight.

It is not coercion with guns. It is **financially blackmail**ed by technocratic language and diplomatic smiles.

And the people? They suffer the consequences of decisions they never had a chance to debate.

Conclusion: The Illusion of Legislative Power

A government that cannot fund education, protect its currency, or control its resources is not sovereign. Moreover, a parliament that cannot write a budget free from foreign approval is not governing. It is **administering austerity on behalf of others**.

Until debt is confronted as a form of domination, democracy will remain a ritual. Until people are allowed to choose leaders who can break contracts that harm them, elections will remain **ceremonial** rather than transformational.

Moreover, the chamber where laws are passed will remain an echo chamber, echoing the terms set by banks far away.

Works Cited

Stiglitz, Joseph. *Globalization and Its Discontents*. W.W. Norton, 2002.
Mkandawire, Thandika. "Adjustment, Political Conditionality and Democratisation in Africa." *Nordic Journal of African Studies*, vol. 4, no. 2, 1995.
Kilani, Mondher. "Tunisia's Democracy and the Debt Trap." *Middle East Eye*, 2020.
International Monetary Fund. *Tunisia Country Report*, No. 21/45, 2021.
Cheru, Fantu. *The Silent Revolution in Africa: Debt, Development, and Democracy*. Zed Books, 1989.

V. Puppet Leaders and "Friendly Strongmen"

When Loyalty Matters More Than Legitimacy

You do not always need a gun to install a regime. Sometimes, all it takes is a handshake and a photo op between a president and a general, a donor and a despot, a diplomat and a puppet who knows precisely what lines he has been hired to recite.

In today's global order, you do not have to crush a democracy to control it. You must **choose the right face**, one that knows how to smile at the camera while signing away national dignity behind closed doors.

These are the **"friendly strongmen"**, leaders who dress in civilian clothes, win rigged elections, and speak the language of reform, but serve not the people, only power. Moreover, time and again, their grip is sustained not by grassroots support but by **foreign approval**.

They wear the mask of democracy, but they answer to the empire.

The Rise of the Puppet Elite

In many U.S.-backed democracies, leaders are selected less for their vision and more for their willingness to **stay in line**:

- To support Western military operations in the region.
- To **open markets to foreign investment**.
- To **vote a certain way at the United Nations**.
- To **host foreign military bases without local consent**.
- To **maintain neoliberal orthodoxy**, no matter the social cost.

Their reward?

- Preferential trade deals.
- Military assistance.
- PR campaigns in Western media.

- Diplomatic immunity for their abuse.

Their punishment for deviation?

- Sanctions.
- Leaked scandals.
- Color revolutions.
- Regime change.

This is not democracy. It is **clientelism in a suit and tie**.

Case Study: Paul Biya, Cameroon's Eternal President

Paul Biya has been the President of Cameroon since 1982. He has been elected and re-elected in a series of contested polls, amid accusations of fraud, repression, and constitutional manipulation.

He spends more time in Swiss hotels than in his capital. Opposition leaders are harassed, jailed, or disappeared. The Anglophone crisis has left thousands dead and displaced.

However, Biya remains a key ally of the U.S. and France in the region, primarily due to his cooperation on counterterrorism and access to Cameroon's resources.

- He receives U.S. military support.
- He maintains cordial relations with international lenders.
- He ensures "stability", a code word for compliance.

The price? A broken nation. The reward? Continued reign.

(Cheeseman, 2018; International Crisis Group, 2022)

Case Study: Faure Gnassingbé, A Dynasty in Democracy's Clothing

Togo has been ruled by the same family since 1967. When Faure Gnassingbé took over after his father died in 2005, it was hailed as a "peaceful transition."

Peaceful, for whom?

- The military installed him despite mass protests.
- Allegations of fraud marred elections.
- Opposition leaders were routinely silenced.

However, Faure remains a "partner" in regional diplomacy and economic liberalization. Why? Because he supports France's military presence, signs World Bank agreements, and keeps Togo "open for business."

The dynasty thrives. People suffocate. Moreover, democracy becomes **a rubber stamp for the monarchy.**

Case Study: Hamid Karzai, Governor in Presidential Garb

In post-invasion Afghanistan, Hamid Karzai was marketed as the "face of a new Afghanistan."

- He spoke fluent English.
- He wore traditional robes for Western cameras.
- He promised modernization.

His actual job was to handle foreign interests.

- Approve oil pipelines.
- Maintain U.S. military presence.
- Suppress independent nationalist movements.
- Endorse IMF-backed reforms in exchange for aid.

He ruled from the Green Zone. Outside it, warlords-controlled territory. The Taliban grew stronger, and public trust collapsed.

When Karzai left office, Afghans referred to him not as a president, but as a **"shadow emir of American design."**

(Scheuer, 2004; Rashid, 2021)

The Problem Is not just the Leader, It is the System That Rewards Them

These men are not exceptions. They are products of a system designed to **filter out independent voices** and reward the compliant:

- Pan-Africanist leaders are undermined.
- Indigenous movements are infiltrated.
- Reformers who reject IMF deals are painted as unstable.
- Anti-imperial activists are labeled extremists.

Meanwhile, those who uphold foreign policy priorities, even if they trample their people, are declared "mature democracies."

Democracy becomes not the rule of the people, but the rule of the agreeable.

Why People Turn Away

Eventually, people see through the charade.

They see that voting does not remove the strongman. The constitutions are rewritten for dynasties. That "reforms" serve donors, not the poor. That parliaments are filled with puppets and cronies, not patriots.

Thus, they rebel.

- Not always through revolution.
- Sometimes through apathy.
- Sometimes through silence.
- Sometimes through the dangerous embrace of militarism.

Not because they reject democracy, but because **what they're offered is a parody of it**.

Conclusion: We Know Our Leaders Do Not Lead

Democracy without sovereignty creates **a theater of obedience**, where leaders are selected not for courage, but for compliance. Where parliaments pass laws, they do not write; where presidents deliver speeches drafted in foreign embassies.

The people know. They always know. Moreover, eventually, they stop clapping.

Because a puppet may wear a sash. Nevertheless, it cannot carry a nation.

Works Cited

Cheeseman, Nic. *How to Rig an Election*. Yale University Press, 2018.

International Crisis Group. *Cameroon: Confronting Anglophone Grievances*. ICG Report No. 250, 2022.

Rashid, Ahmed. *Descent Into Chaos*. Viking, 2021.

Scheuer, Michael. *Imperial Hubris: Why the West Is Losing the War on Terror*. Potomac Books, 2004.

Amnesty International. *Togo: Repression and Renewed Protests*. 2019.

VI. Sovereignty Interrupted, When Civil Society Becomes a Foreign Asset

The NGO That Speaks Louder Than the People

In theory, civil society is the soul of democracy. It is where voices gather when institutions fail, where protest becomes policy, where the powerless find platforms.

What occurs when that soul is purchased?

Across the Global South, NGOs, once rooted in struggle, sacrifice, and local accountability, have increasingly become **franchises of foreign interests**. They arrive with grants, mission statements, and frameworks.

They bring laptops, T-shirts, and data dashboards. However, often, what they leave behind is something else entirely: **a politics of dependency**.

The people speak, but in someone else's vocabulary. They resist, but within the limits of donor expectations. They build, but only on terrain pre-approved by embassies.

This is **sovereignty interrupted**, not by thanks or trade agreements, but by **civil society that serves another flag**.

The Aid Trap for Activism

The logic seems innocent enough:
"You have problems. We have funds. Let us partner."

However, under that surface lie power dynamics that distort movements:

- Budgets dictate ideology.
- Funding cycles shape strategy.
- "Results" are measured in grant reports, not community transformation.
- Local organizers become "project officers."
- Consultants replace elders.
- Dissent becomes **development speaking**.

Moreover, soon, activism is less about **mobilizing people** and more about **pleasing donors**.

The fight for liberation is rewritten as a **logframe**.

Case Study: Haiti, NGOs as Parallel Government

After the 2010 earthquake, the world pledged over $13 billion in aid to rebuild Haiti. However, more than 90% of that money never reached Haitian institutions.

Instead, it was routed through:

- International NGOs.
- Foreign contractors.
- Donor-country development agencies.

These organizations operated with little oversight, often duplicating efforts, sidelining local expertise, and creating a **"second government"** that had money, but no accountability to Haitian citizens.

The result?

- Communities left out of planning.
- Government capacity hollowed out.
- Haitian civil society groups are drowned out by louder, more affluent foreign counterparts.

As Haitian scholar Jean-Claude Jean put it:

"We were no longer rebuilding Haiti, we were rebuilding the image of Western benevolence." (*The Guardian*, 2015)

Case Study: Sudan, The Fragmented Revolution

In 2019, after decades of dictatorship, Sudanese protesters toppled Omar al-Bashir. Civil society was hailed as the hero of the revolution.

During the subsequent transition, foreign actors hurried to finance and influence the emerging landscape.

- "Youth empowerment" programs replaced political education.
- Entrepreneurship training took precedence over grassroots organizing.
- U.S. and European donors favored groups that embraced neoliberal economic reforms, sidelining leftist and Pan-African movements.

Instead of building a sovereign civil society, the transition became **a laboratory for imported democracy**, severed from the revolutionary energy that had made it possible.

By 2021, the military had regained power.

The people led the revolution. Nevertheless, **the consultants ran the transition**.

(Stewart, "Sudan's Stolen Democracy," *Foreign Policy*, 2022)

The Birth of the NGO Class

A new elite has emerged in many "developing democracies", **the NGO class**:

- Educated abroad.
- Fluent in donor language.
- Traveling from one conference to the next.
- Familiar with Western foundations yet disconnected from local realities.

This class often becomes the **bridge between foreign power and domestic legitimacy**. However, it also becomes a gatekeeper, filtering which movements receive attention, which are dismissed, and which are funded.

Moreover, those who do not conform? Branded as "radical," "uncivil," and "undemocratic."

The Consequences of Outsourced Dissent

When civil society is externally funded and directed, several consequences follow:

1. **Co-optation**: Real movements are tamed into projects.
2. **Fragmentation**: Communities compete for funding instead of uniting.

3. **Legitimacy Crisis**: Citizens stop trusting activists who prioritize speaking to donors over their neighbors.
4. **Surveillance by Proxy**: NGO staff often unknowingly serve as intelligence conduits, collecting data on political activity under the guise of "monitoring."

Over time, the line between democracy and dependency becomes increasingly blurred.

Conclusion: We Want Our Voices Back

Civil society must be vibrant, fierce, and fearless. However, it cannot be outsourced. It cannot speak in scripts written in foreign capitals. Moreover, it cannot serve people; it never consults.

Until the Global South reclaims its movements from the grip of donor agendas and the soft coercion of aid, democracy will remain a contract, not a covenant.

Because a voice that only echoes its funders is not a voice of the people. It is **an asset, not an advocate**.

Works Cited

Belloni, Roberto. *The Rise and Fall of International Civil Society Assistance*. Oxford University Press, 2020.

Schuller, Mark. *Killing with Kindness: Haiti, International Aid, and NGOs*. Rutgers University Press, 2012.

Jean, Jean-Claude. "Why Haiti's NGOs Failed the People." *The Guardian*, 2015.

Stewart, Emily. "Sudan's Stolen Democracy." *Foreign Policy*, March 2022.

Mkandawire, Thandika. "African Intellectuals and the Politics of Civil Society." *CODESRIA Bulletin*, 2002.

Prashad, Vijay. *The Poorer Nations: A Possible History of the Global South*.

Verso, 2013.

VII. When Voters Lose Faith, The Backlash to Hollow Democracy

Disillusionment, Defiance, and the Rise of the Irregular

There is a certain silence more dangerous than protest: the silence of a voter who does not show up, of a citizen who no longer believes the ballot counts, of a young person who trades dreams of public service for the fire of insurgency, and of a nation where hope recedes, not in rage, but in resignation.

This is the legacy of hollow democracies: a culture of **disbelief, detachment, and defiance**.

It is not that people have stopped believing in democracy. It is that democracy, **as they have lived it**, gave up on them first.

The Collapse of Civic Faith

Across many nations in the Global South, participation in elections has dropped sharply:

- In **Nigeria**, less than 30% of registered voters participated in the 2023 presidential election, **the lowest in the country's democratic history**.
- In **Haiti**, elections are postponed indefinitely amid gang violence and a political vacuum, **not from apathy, but from the complete collapse of institutional credibility**.
- In **Tunisia**, youth turnout in recent referenda dropped below 15%, a direct response to IMF-imposed austerity and an unresponsive political elite.

These are not isolated trends. They are **cries of exhaustion**.

People have watched "democracy" deliver:

- Cut pensions and raise fuel costs.

- Foreign military bases and privatized hospitals.
- Corrupt elites praised abroad for their "stability."
- Empty gestures while real decisions are made elsewhere.

What began as a belief turned into betrayal. Moreover, betrayal breeds **backlash**.

Case Study: Mali, Niger, and Burkina Faso, The Military Steps In

In West Africa, a wave of military coups has shaken the region:

- **Mali** (2020 & 2021)
- **Guinea** (2021)
- **Burkina Faso** (2022)
- **Niger** (2023)

Western leaders and institutions condemned the coups. However, within each country, thousands flooded the streets **to celebrate** the soldiers. Protesters waved Russian and Pan-African flags, burned French symbols, and called the new leaders "liberators."

Why?

Because the democratically elected governments they replaced were seen as:

- Complicit in foreign exploitation.
- Inept at ending insecurity.
- Submissive to IMF austerity and French neocolonial influence.
- Detached from the daily suffering of their people.

In the minds of many, the coup was not an attack on democracy. It was **a correction of its betrayal**.

(Baché, 2023; Tchérina, *African Security Review*)

When Populism Fills the Vacuum

Elsewhere, the loss of faith in liberal democratic structures has fueled the rise of:

- **Strongman populists** who promise to "take back control."
- **Religious extremism** offers moral clarity amid corruption.
- **Ethno-nationalist movements** that scapegoat minorities and outsiders.

Each of these grows in soil fertilized by **democratic disappointment**.

When people see elites co-opted, NGOs funded by foreign interests, and votes that yield no change, they seek meaning in more extreme alternatives, not because they are irrational, but because **rational hope has run dry**.

Youth: Hope and the Heartbreak

Perhaps the most heartbreaking dimension of democratic failure is its impact on the youth.

- Young people in Lebanon, Zimbabwe, Sudan, and Sri Lanka have taken to the streets repeatedly.
- They organize, educate, agitate, but are met with bullets, broken promises, or donor-co-opted "dialogue."
- Over time, some withdraw. Others radicalize. Many leave **brain drains driven not by poverty alone, but by political despair**.

In Tunisia, a university graduate explained to a journalist:

"We voted, we protested, we built coalitions. However, the IMF still oversees our budget, and the same individuals remain in the ministries. This is not my revolution anymore."

(*Al Jazeera*, 2021)

Democracy Has a Smell, and the People Know When It is Rotten

True democracy smells like agency, dignity, and consequence. False democracy smells like **recycled policies, scripted parliaments, and economic orders you did not choose**.

Moreover, the people, especially the poor, the young, the rural, the dispossessed, can smell the difference.

So, they stop clapping. They stop voting. Alternatively, they vote with their feet, their fists, their faith in something new.

Conclusion: You Cannot Fool the Wounded Forever

There comes a moment when a person, long fooled, stops playing along.

They stopped attending the performance. They stopped believing that the next candidate would change the script. They begin, slowly and suddenly, to write **a new one**.

Sometimes it is hopeful. Sometimes it is reckless. It always starts in the same place: with the understanding that what they were told was that democracy was nothing more than an empty shell.

Once people realize the house is hollow, they stop trying to rearrange the furniture. They begin searching for the exit or matches.

Works Cited

Baché, Emmanuel. "Why People Are Celebrating Coups in West Africa." *The Conversation*, 2023.

Tchérina, Bénédicte. "Civil-Military Relations and Sovereignty in the Sahel." *African Security Review*, vol. 31, no. 2, 2023.

Al Jazeera. "Tunisia's Youth: The Revolution Is Over." *Al Jazeera English*, August 2021.

Cheeseman, Nic. *Democracy in Africa: Successes, Failures, and the Struggle for Political Reform*. Cambridge University Press, 2015.

Mkandawire, Thandika. "Disempowering the Poor: The Politics of Neoliberal Reform." *Development and Change*, 1999.

VIII. Reclaiming Sovereignty: Pathways Beyond the Puppet Show

From Imported Scripts to Indigenous Power

There is a point in every awakening when the fog begins to lift. When people realize the applause they have been taught to seek is not freedom, but validation from a distant audience. When leaders who once paraded as saviors are exposed as **managers of borrowed power**. Moreover, when "civil society," "elections," and "reform" no longer sedate the hunger for **self-rule**.

We are living in such a moment.

Across the Global South, from the hills of Bolivia to the streets of Khartoum, from Accra's academic halls to Nairobi's slums, a new generation is rising, not to reject democracy, but to **redefine it**.

This section is not a conclusion. It is an invitation: To reclaim democracy not as imitation, but as inheritance. To rebuild sovereignty not as isolation, but as **dignified interdependence**.

Reclaiming the Right to Say "No"

True sovereignty begins with the ability to **refuse**.

- To reject military bases that do not serve your people.
- To refuse aid tied to austerity or ideological conditioning.
- To say no to trade agreements that undermine local farmers and workers.
- To cancel debts incurred under corrupt regimes or exploitative terms.

This is not defiance. It is **responsible leadership**.

As Thomas Sankara once declared before the Organization of African Unity in 1987:

"Debt is a cleverly managed reconquest of Africa. It is a new form of slavery." (*Thomas Sankara Speaks*, Pathfinder Press)

To reclaim sovereignty, a nation must reclaim its **right to refuse subjugation disguised as partnership**.

Localizing Democracy, Power That Speaks the People's Language

Democracy cannot be copy-pasted. It must be grown.

That means rooting political systems in **indigenous knowledge**, **spiritual traditions**, **oral governance structures**, and **grassroots accountability**:

- In **Senegal**, village elders still mediate justice long before courts intervene.
- In **Bolivia**, the constitution enshrines **plurinational democracy**, recognizing the sovereignty of Aymara and Quechua peoples.
- In **India**, local *panchayat* systems offer decentralized decision-making rooted in history, not bureaucracy.

These models may not look like Westminster or Washington. However, they **work** because they reflect the soul of the people.

Sovereignty means not just choosing your leaders but also choosing how you choose them.

Pan-African and South–South Solidarity

No nation reclaims sovereignty alone. It takes alliances rooted in **shared trauma and shared hope**.

Across the Global South, a quiet revolution is underway:

- **The African Continental Free Trade Area (AfCFTA)** seeks to bypass neocolonial trade dependencies.
- **The BRICS+ alliance** challenges Western economic hegemony and offers alternatives to the IMF/World Bank model.

- Movements like **ALBA**, **CELAC**, and **ASEAN** foster regional resilience through political coordination and cultural affirmation.

This is not nostalgia for the Cold War. It is **a blueprint for multipolar dignity**.

Reclaiming sovereignty means choosing **our neighbors** over our former masters.

Debt Justice and Economic Independence

You cannot govern with empty pockets, and debt has become the leash on most "independent" nations.

Nevertheless, that is changing:

- **Zambia** became the first African country to default during COVID-19 and is now calling for multilateral debt restructuring, **on its terms**.
- **Argentina** pushed back against IMF loan conditions and won concessions through mass mobilization.
- **Ecuador's Rafael Correa** declared portions of the country's debt "illegitimate" and refused to pay, sparking a global conversation about **odious debt**.

This is what reclaiming sovereignty looks like: Not refusal for its own sake, but for **economic justice**.

The Role of Conscious Leadership

Movements alone cannot replace systems. They must **birth leaders** who:

- Serve the people, not foreign consultants.
- See the village before they see the visa.
- Speak their mother tongue without shame.
- Prioritize sovereignty over applause.

These leaders are rising. They may not yet sit in presidential palaces, but they walk in classrooms, on farms, in labor unions, and on local councils.

They know that democracy is not built by mimicry, but by memory, struggle, and sacrifice.

Moreover, they are teaching a new lesson:

That **dignity is a better currency than dependency**.

Conclusion: The End of the Puppet Show

The curtain has fallen. The applause has died down. The actors no longer recite their lines.

Across the world, people are tired of performing democracy. They want to **live it**.

They want systems they shape, leaders they choose, economies they control, and futures that answer only to their children.

This chapter ends where it began: with truth.

That a parliament without sovereignty is not a parliament. That democracy without agency is performance. Moreover, the people, once awakened, will not go quietly back into the audience.

Works Cited

Sankara, Thomas. *Thomas Sankara Speaks: The Burkina Faso Revolution 1983–87*. Pathfinder Press, 2007.

Amin, Samir. *The Liberal Virus: Permanent War and the Americanization of the World*. Monthly Review Press, 2004.

Prashad, Vijay. *The Poorer Nations: A Possible History of the Global South*. Verso, 2013.

Mkandawire, Thandika. *Beyond Political Conditionality*. Nordic Africa Institute, 1999.

United Nations Economic Commission for Africa. *AfCFTA and Africa's Sovereign Agenda*, 2021.

Joseph, Gilbert M. "Sovereignty and Social Justice in the New Latin American Left." *Latin American*

Chapter 5 Recap: Puppets and Parliaments, Democracy Without Sovereignty

Staged Elections, Imported Constitutions, and the Illusion of Choice

Chapter 5 delivers a scathing but sober truth: the performance of Democracy, when lacking sovereignty, is not true democracy; it becomes theater. Through a thorough examination of post-colonial states and U.S.-backed transitions, the chapter exposes the polished facade of "free" nations' parliaments, presidents, and constitutions, revealing the **invisible hand of foreign control** that governs from behind the curtain.

The central argument is direct: **democracy without the power to choose one's path is an illusion.** Moreover, country after country, people are waking up to that fact.

Key Themes and Arguments

1. The Spectacle of Self-Governance

- Nations are celebrated for holding elections and passing constitutions, but the core decisions, about debt, defense, and development, are dictated elsewhere.
- Governance becomes a stage performance where sovereignty is sacrificed for legitimacy in the eyes of foreign patrons.

2. The Illusion of Choice

- Elections offer multiple parties but no genuine alternative to neoliberal economic orthodoxy or geopolitical alignment with the West.

- In places like Afghanistan, Nigeria, and Haiti, disillusionment deepens because voting **does not equal agency**.

3. Constitutions as Contracts

- Instead of being rooted in culture or struggle, many constitutions are ghostwritten by Western consultants, embedded with clauses that serve capital, not citizens.
- Iraq, Kenya, and other nations have been handed founding documents designed to lock in neoliberalism and decentralize power to keep national governments weak and compliant.

4. Debt as a Cage

- Countries like Ghana and Tunisia are trapped in cycles of IMF debt and austerity, unable to make independent policy choices without punishment.
- Parliaments lose the power of the purse. Budgets are drafted not for people, but for creditors.

5. Puppet Leaders and Friendly Strongmen

- The U.S. and its allies often back elites who protect foreign interests, regardless of their repression at home.
- Leaders like Paul Biya, Faure Gnassingbé, and Hamid Karzai are presented as democratic partners while operating as gatekeepers of imperial interests.

6. Civil Society as a Trojan Horse

- NGOs, once engines of resistance, are increasingly funded, framed, and filtered by Western donors.
- In Haiti and Sudan, this has led to the hollowing out of grassroots activism and the rise of a new NGO class that is more accountable to embassies than to citizens.

7. Backlash and Disillusionment

- Across the world, hollow democracy is giving rise to coups, populism, voter apathy, and political instability, not because people reject democracy, but because **they have never experienced the real thing**.
- In Mali, Niger, and Burkina Faso, military regimes enjoy public support because elected governments were perceived as being foreign-controlled and domestically unresponsive.

8. Reclaiming Sovereignty

The chapter closes with a blueprint for moving beyond the puppet show:

- **Saying no** to aid with strings.
- **Localizing democracy** in indigenous systems.
- **Rebuilding regional alliances** and South–South solidarity.
- **Rejecting debt dependency** and neoliberal austerity.
- **Raising new leaders** from within communities, not from donor shortlists.

Real democracy, the chapter insists, is not built on borrowed constitutions or imported parties. It is grown, rooted in culture, watered by struggle, and sustained by sovereignty.

Final Reflection

Chapter 5 is a call to stop clapping for parliaments that cannot legislate.

It asks us to abandon the fantasy that elections alone make a country free. Moreover, most of all, it demands that we **listen to the silences**, those quiet rooms where real decisions are made, far from voting booths and public squares.

Until people can write their laws, fund their futures, and reject external control without punishment, **the democratic theater will remain just that stage.**

However, the audience is getting restless. The actors have forgotten their lines. Furthermore, outside, people are beginning to build a new set with their own hands.

Chapter 6:

The IMF and World Bank, Economic Shackles in Diplomatic Clothing

When Aid Becomes Architecture for Dependence

They came wearing the garments of salvation.

The International Monetary Fund and the World Bank, born out of the wreckage of World War II, entered the post-colonial world stage not as colonizers, but as "partners." They offered lifelines. Loans. Technical expertise. Advice. They carried the flag of development, spoke the language of poverty reduction, and preached the gospel of global integration.

What they offered, in truth, was not liberation; it was a contract. One written in the fine print of interest rates, conditionalities, and structural adjustments. For much of the Global South, signing that contract was not an act of choice, but of necessity, coercion, or inherited crisis.

This chapter is not about numbers and charts. It is about power dressed as assistance. It is about the quiet violence of policies that look neutral on paper but extract life in practice. It is about how the two most influential financial institutions in the world have transformed economic help into a **chokehold**, one that disciplines nations into obedience, erodes sovereignty, and institutionalizes global inequality under the banner of reform.

The Origins of the Machinery: Bretton Woods Was Never for Us

In July 1944, delegates from 44 nations met in Bretton Woods, New Hampshire, to imagine a new world order. The devastation of war had made clear the need for global financial coordination. Out of that conference came two twins: the International Monetary Fund (IMF) and the International Bank for Reconstruction and Development, known as the World Bank.

Their purpose? Stabilize currencies. Rebuild Europe. Facilitate investment.

While Europe was being rebuilt, colonies were still being exploited. The economies of Africa, Asia, and Latin America were not designed for sovereignty; they were extraction engines. The IMF and World Bank, whether by design or by evolution, became the **custodians of that engine**.

Though many nations participated in the Bretton Woods talks, the final structure of these institutions gave **voting power based on financial contribution**. The result: the United States, and to a lesser extent Europe, would dominate the decision-making tables. Even today, the U.S. holds de facto veto power in both institutions.

So, when independence movements swept the Global South in the mid-20th century, newly sovereign nations found themselves financially dependent on an international system built by their former colonizers and run by their current creditors.

Structural Adjustment: The Gospel of Austerity

By the late 1970s and early 1980s, economic crises gripped much of the Global South. Oil shocks, currency devaluations, and inherited colonial debts brought countries to the brink. The IMF and World Bank stepped in, not with unconditional relief, but with **conditions**.

Thus began the era of **Structural Adjustment Programs** (SAPs), a euphemism for enforced neoliberalism.

These programs followed a familiar pattern:

- **Privatize state-owned enterprises**, from water to railways, from hospitals to power grids.
- **Slash social spending**, cutting subsidies for food, fuel, and education.

- **Deregulate markets**, allowing foreign capital to flood in and dominate.
- **Devalue national currencies**, making exports cheaper, but imports (and life) more expensive.
- **Focus on debt repayment over development**, redirecting resources from clinics to creditors.

These weren't recommendations. They were **preconditions for loans**.

And the consequences were devastating.

The Human Cost: From Textbook Theory to Starving Households

In Ghana, SAPs led to tuition fees in public schools and "cash-and-carry" hospital policies, meaning you paid before treatment, or you were left to die.

In Zambia, copper mines were privatized, thousands were laid off, and the national economy was gutted. The profits? They flowed to foreign shareholders. The debt? It remained with the people.

In Jamaica, IMF policies led to frozen wages, rising food costs, and public sector layoffs, fueling unrest that has still not fully subsided.

And in Bolivia, the World Bank helped orchestrate the privatization of the water system in Cochabamba. Prices skyrocketed. Even rainwater collection became illegal under the new corporate regime. The people revolted. Tear gas filled the streets. The government eventually canceled the contract, but the damage was done.

These are not anomalies. They are case studies in how **"development" becomes dispossession**.

Debt: The Eternal Leash

The tragedy of it all is this: countries borrow not for luxury, but for survival. They borrow to stabilize, to feed, to invest. By the time repayment began, the principal had multiplied. Loans get stacked on loans. The interest payments consume national budgets.

Countries like Mozambique, Senegal, and Pakistan now spend **more on debt service than on health and education combined**.

When do they default? They are punished. Their credit rating drops. Capital flees. New loans come with even stricter conditions.

This is **financial imperialism**, control not by armies, but by balance sheets.

Democracy Undermined by Design

Perhaps the most insidious impact of IMF and World Bank control is how it **undermines political sovereignty**.

What good is an election if the newly elected government cannot pass a budget without approval from Washington or Brussels?

What meaning does democracy have if parliaments are bound by agreements signed by previous administrations or unelected technocrats?

In theory, these institutions are apolitical. In practice, they have **dictated the domestic policies of more countries than any empire in modern history**.

And they've done so behind closed doors, with little transparency, no public debate, and **zero democratic mandate**.

Rebranding Empire: Poverty Reduction and Green Finance

In the 2000s, facing backlash, the IMF and World Bank changed their vocabulary.

They no longer imposed "austerity." They promoted "Poverty Reduction Strategy Papers."

They no longer pushed SAPs. They supported "growth frameworks."

In the 2020s, they speak of climate finance, gender equity, and inclusion.

The structure remains: loans with conditions. Debt with strings. Growth measured in GDP, not in dignity.

Even climate funds are now being disbursed as **loans**, not grants, pushing countries deeper into debt to fight a crisis they didn't create.

Resistance: The South Rises Again

Yet all is not lost.

- Argentina defaulted and refused the IMF terms, then recovered faster than expected.
- Ecuador declared part of its debt "illegitimate" and negotiated on new terms.
- Bolivia kicked out the World Bank-backed water companies.
- BRICS is building alternative financial institutions.
- The African Union is exploring a **Pan-African Monetary Fund**.

People are rising. Movements are forming. A new economics is being imagined, not of extraction, but of equity.

Conclusion: Who Really Owes Whom?

Let us be clear: the Global South is not a debtor. It is a creditor.

It has paid with its minerals, its forests, its people, its sweat.

The IMF and World Bank claim to promote development. Their track record shows a different truth: they have helped maintain a world where the rich get richer, the poor stay indebted, and sovereignty is sacrificed at the altar of creditworthiness.

It is time to stop whispering this truth.

It is time to say plainly: **no system that demands obedience before survival can be called democratic**.

No institution that calls poverty a debt problem, rather than a justice problem, can claim to speak for the future.

Section I: The Bretton Woods Blueprint, A Post-War Economic Order

They met not on the battlefield, but in the hills of New Hampshire, forty-four nations, *scarred* by war, gathered in July 1944 to shape the future. The Nazis had not yet surrendered, and the bombs had not yet stopped falling. The victors were already drawing the lines of a new financial world. The result? A blueprint called Bretton Woods.

The conference itself was draped in diplomacy. Behind the handshakes and signatures were two towering objectives: rebuilding war-torn Europe and stabilizing global trade. At its heart were two freshly conceived institutions, the International Monetary Fund (IMF) and the International Bank for Reconstruction and Development (IBRD), which would later become the World Bank.

Their stated mission? To prevent another Great Depression. To ensure economic cooperation. To assist nations in balancing payments, securing loans, and investing in infrastructure.

Their actual legacy? Something far more complicated, and far more coercive.

From Reconstruction to Control

In its earliest years, the IMF functioned like an emergency room for industrial economies, helping stabilize currencies, smooth out payment imbalances, and keep trade routes open. The World Bank, meanwhile, financed massive infrastructure projects, from dams to highways to power plants, mostly in Europe and later in Japan.

By the 1950s, the Cold War reoriented priorities. Western powers, now led by an assertive United States, saw financial instruments not just as tools of reconstruction, but as levers of ideological warfare. Economic assistance became conditional. Loans were granted not just on merit or need, but on alignment. Markets had to be opened. Governments had to be friendly. Socialism had to be discouraged or dismantled.

Slowly, the purpose of the Bretton Woods institutions shifted, from recovery to **regulation**, not for the powerful, but for the **post-colonial world**.

While Europe was being rebuilt with generous, low-interest loans through the Marshall Plan, newly independent African, Asian, and Latin American countries were subjected to rigorous "reform packages." Their budgets were examined. Their economies were dissected. Their political sovereignty, though newly won, was increasingly mediated through Washington, D.C., where the IMF and World Bank set up headquarters and wrote the rules of development finance.

A Voting System Rigged by Design

In theory, the IMF and World Bank are "international" organizations. Every member country has a vote. Every voice matters.

Look beneath the surface.

Votes are not counted equally. They are weighed based on a nation's financial contribution to the institution's pool, called a quota. And those quotas reflect not population, need, or vulnerability, but wealth.

As of 2025, the United States holds over 16% of the total IMF voting shares. Since major decisions require an 85% supermajority, this gives the U.S. an **effective veto** over all major decisions. Western European countries, Germany, France, and the UK, collectively dominate another third. Meanwhile, the entire continent of Africa, home to 54 countries, holds just around 6%.

It's like being invited to dinner, only to find the menu, the recipes, and the seating chart already decided. And when the bill comes due, it's the poorest guests who must pay with interest.

The result is a structural bias. IMF and World Bank policies, priorities, and leadership reflect the preferences of creditor nations, especially the U.S. They do not emerge from consensus, but from command.

As economic historian Eric Toussaint argues, "The IMF and World Bank are not neutral institutions. They serve the interests of the countries and corporations that dominate them" (The World Bank: A Critical Primer, 2008).

The Myth of Neutrality

What makes the IMF and World Bank particularly dangerous is not just their power, but the illusion of neutrality with which they wield it. Their economists wear suits, not uniforms. Their policies are drafted in "technical" language, not political speeches. Their visits to struggling nations are framed as "missions," not occupations.

The impact is no less profound.

What the IMF calls "fiscal discipline" is, in practice, a slashing of social services. What it labels "public sector reform" is the mass firing of teachers, nurses, and civil servants. What is termed "currency realignment" often leads to inflation, unrest, and hunger.

The language may be sanitized, but the consequences are lived by mothers who walk miles for now-privatized water, by children turned away from overcrowded clinics, by farmers priced out of their land.

This is not neutral. It is **policy violence** dressed in spreadsheets.

Bretton Woods and the Global South: An Inheritance of Exclusion

Most countries in the Global South did not attend Bretton Woods as equals. Many were still under colonial rule. Their economies were not designed to thrive, but to supply raw materials to foreign markets. When independence finally arrived, so did the bills, from colonial debt to trade deficits.

The IMF and World Bank stepped in not to transform this legacy, but to **manage** it. To make it sustainable for creditors. To prevent collapse, not for the people, but for the global economic order.

So, the blueprint of Bretton Woods became an **architecture of dependence**.

Even today, when crises strike, be it financial, pandemic, or climate, the IMF and World Bank are first responders. Their help comes with old logic: open your markets, cut your budget, deregulate your economy.

They call it reform. People call it robbery.

Conclusion: The Blueprints Were Never Meant to Free Us

Bretton Woods was never a plan for universal prosperity. It was a design for **stability under Western leadership**. It was meant to rebuild the world, but only parts of it. It created order, but only for some.

The Global South did not draw the map. We have been made to walk it. Blindfolded. And in circles.

To understand the role of the IMF and World Bank today, we must return to their original stories because power is not just in the policies. It is on the premises. Until those premises are rewritten by the people they once excluded, the roar of financial freedom will remain just another myth echoing through the halls of empire.

Works Cited (MLA)

Toussaint, Eric. The World Bank: A Critical Primer. Pluto Press, 2008.

Stiglitz, Joseph E. Globalization and Its Discontents. W.W. Norton & Company, 2002.

Hickel, Jason. The Divide: Global Inequality from Conquest to Free Markets. W.W. Norton, 2017.

Peet, Richard. Unholy Trinity: The IMF, World Bank, and WTO. Zed Books, 2009.

Kentikelenis, Alexander, et al. "Structural Adjustment and Health: A Conceptual Framework and Evidence on Pathways." Social Science & Medicine, vol. 187, 2017, pp. 296–305.

Section II: Structural Adjustment, The Austerity Gospel

How the IMF Preached Discipline While Spreading Dependency

There was a time when debt came with dignity, when borrowing was understood as a bridge to sovereignty, not a surrender of it. By the early 1980s, the language around international lending had changed. Loans were no longer simply financial transactions. They became instruments of **ideological transmission**, vehicles for restructuring entire societies in the name of "efficiency," "fiscal discipline," and "modernization."

This shift gave birth to one of the most destructive economic frameworks of the modern age: the **Structural Adjustment Program**, or SAP.

Marketed as a cure for chronic underdevelopment, SAPs promised to help indebted nations "adjust" to global financial realities. In truth, they imposed a one-size-fits-all model of economic austerity and market liberalization, crafted not in African parliaments or Latin American assemblies, but in the boardrooms of Washington D.C.

These were not suggestions. They were **non-negotiable conditions**, tied to IMF and World Bank loans, imposed during moments of desperation, and implemented with minimal input from the people most affected.

The Core Tenets of Structural Adjustment

Across continents and cultures, the SAPs followed a disturbingly familiar script:

1. Currency devaluation to promote exports but often triggers inflation and wipes out local purchasing power.
2. Privatization of state-owned enterprises, transferring essential services to profit-driven corporations.
3. Liberalization of trade, allowing cheap imports to flood local markets and destroy domestic industries.

4. Elimination of subsidies, particularly on food, fuel, and health, hits the poor hardest.
5. Drastic cuts to public spending, leading to underfunded schools, hospitals, and public sector layoffs.

SAPs were never just economic policies; they were acts of **economic reengineering**, often done without public consultation and in violation of national constitutions.

"These programs were essentially the same everywhere. They failed, everywhere." Joseph E. Stiglitz, Globalization and Its Discontents (Norton, 2002)

Case Study 1: Ghana, Austerity and the Death of Public Welfare

In the early 1980s, Ghana was in crisis, with rising inflation, collapsing export prices, and mounting debt. The IMF stepped in with a structural adjustment package hailed as a "model" for Africa.

What followed was a textbook SAP:

- The cedi was devalued by over 1000%.
- Price controls were lifted.
- Hundreds of state enterprises were privatized.
- Food and fuel subsidies were slashed.
- Health and education budgets were gutted.

Ghanaians paid for this reform with their bodies. Under "cash and carry" healthcare, patients were required to pay upfront before receiving treatment, even for emergencies. Maternal and infant mortality spiked. Education enrollment dropped. Hunger increased.

The economy grew on paper, but **real people were dying**.

A 1989 World Bank evaluation proudly reported that Ghana had achieved macroeconomic "stability." It said nothing about the women giving birth on clinic floors, the malnourished children dropping out of school, or the civil servants who could no longer afford food on their salaries.

"They told us the economy had healed. What they healed was the investor's confidence, not the patient.", former Ghanaian civil servant (Author Interview, 2019)

Case Study 2: Jamaica, No Way Out

Jamaica began borrowing from the IMF in the late 1970s. By the 1980s, it was fully embedded in SAPs. Despite decades of loans, Jamaica found itself trapped in a cycle of dependency:

- Wages were frozen.
- Government hiring was restricted.
- Import liberalization flooded markets with U.S. agricultural goods, decimating local farmers.
- Export earnings were increasingly diverted to repay debt.

One of the most poignant consequences was education. Schools in rural areas crumbled as budgets were slashed. Basic supplies, like chalk, books, and even toilet paper, became luxuries.

By 2010, Jamaica's debt-to-GDP ratio had ballooned past 140%, despite years of "reform." Its economy had stagnated for decades.

Michael Manley, a former Jamaican Prime Minister, once described SAPs as a "political straitjacket disguised as economics."

"They called it aid, but it came with a leash, and the tighter we pulled, the more it choked us." Jamaican economist Clive Thomas, Debt and Development (2008)

Case Study 3: Zambia, Copper, Cuts, and Collapse

Zambia's economy, once buoyed by copper exports, plummeted in the 1980s. The IMF stepped in, demanding SAPs as the price of assistance.

- The kwacha was devalued repeatedly.

- Public services were cut to the bone.
- State mines were privatized at bargain-basement prices.
- User fees were introduced for health and education.

By the mid-1990s, over 10,000 workers had been laid off. With no safety nets, communities descended into poverty. Waterborne diseases surged. Child labor increased. HIV/AIDS rates soared.

The World Bank praised Zambia for being a "strong reformer." Meanwhile, the country's GDP per capita fell, and its debt only deepened.

In 2006, Zambians took to the streets, demanding accountability, not just from their government, but from the IMF itself.

"They dismantled our economy, then blamed us for being poor." Zambian union leader quoted in Looting Africa by Patrick Bond (Zed Books, 2006)

SAPs: Success Measured by Suffering

Across the Global South, SAPs created a paradox. They produced **macroeconomic indicators** that pleased lenders: controlled inflation, reduced deficits, and expanded trade.

They also generated **human suffering** on a scale rarely acknowledged in donor reports.

In Kenya, over 400,000 public workers were laid off. In Nigeria, SAPs exacerbated inequality and triggered riots. In Bolivia, they sowed the seeds of a populist backlash that would bring Evo Morales to power.

The common thread? SAPs shrunk the state, not corruption. They slashed services, not subsidies to elites. They opened economies but closed futures.

Conclusion: A Gospel Without Grace

To call structural adjustment a "gospel" is not hyperbole; it was preached with the zeal of missionaries and imposed with the rigidity of dogma. It promised salvation just over the next loan cycle.

Unlike gospel, SAPs offered no grace. No forgiveness. No path to redemption.

They turned public health into a budget line. They turned democracy into conditionality. They turned entire nations into fiscal laboratories, places where ideology was tested, regardless of cost.

Through it all, the same hands held the pen. The same institutions issued grades. The same people paid the price.

Works Cited (MLA)

Bond, Patrick. Looting Africa: The Economics of Exploitation. Zed Books, 2006.

Harrison, Graham. The World Bank and Africa: The Construction of Governance States. Routledge, 2004.

Manley, Michael. Jamaica: Struggle in the Periphery. Howard University Press, 1982.

Stiglitz, Joseph E. Globalization and Its Discontents. W.W. Norton & Company, 2002.

Toussaint, Eric. The World Bank: A Critical Primer. Pluto Press, 2008.

Section III: Debt as Leverage, Modern-Day Vassalage

How Loans Become Chains, and Sovereignty Is Bought in Installments

In the feudal world of old, kings and emperors ruled by sword and decree. They collected tribute, enforced obedience, and reminded the peasantry that loyalty was not optional; it was the cost of survival. Today, the sword has been replaced by spreadsheets, and tribute comes not in grain but in interest payments. The sovereigns now wear suits in Washington. Their palaces are named the IMF and the World Bank.

In this modern age of diplomacy and development, **debt is the new dominion**.

The countries of the Global South, already burdened by the legacies of colonization, were told that independence would be followed by prosperity. They were told they would "catch up." The road to development was paved with loans, investments, and partnerships.

What they received was not a partnership. It was a contract signed during a crisis, enforced with conditionalities, and monitored through quarterly reviews. Loans that promised lifelines became **leashes**. Every repayment reinforced a structure of dependence where sovereignty was not extinguished but mortgaged.

The Cycle of Entrapment

The mechanics of modern debt are deceptively simple:

1. A country borrows to cover a budget deficit, finance development, or stabilize its currency.
2. That loan accrues interest, often more rapidly than the economy grows.
3. When repayment is due, the country lacks reserves.
4. So, it borrows again, from the IMF, World Bank, or other creditors, just to stay afloat.
5. Each new loan comes with deeper conditions, stricter fiscal ceilings, and less policy space.

This is the **trap**. Borrow to survive and lose the power to decide.

As Jason Hickel writes, "Debt is not just about money, it's about power. It's about who controls whom, and on what terms" (The Divide, Norton, 2017).

Case Study: Haiti, Independence, Paid in Blood and Interest

Haiti won its independence in 1804, defeating one of the world's most powerful empires. France demanded compensation, **not for damages, but for "lost property"**: the formerly enslaved population.

In 1825, under threat of invasion, Haiti agreed to pay France 150 million francs (later reduced to 90 million), a debt that would take over a century to repay. To meet the payments, Haiti had to borrow from French and U.S. banks, thus beginning its prolonged entrapment in a debt cycle that crushed development before it could begin.

Fast forward to the 20th century, Haiti became a regular borrower from the IMF. Loans arrived with the usual conditions: privatize utilities, reduce tariffs, cut social spending. In 2000, the IMF pushed for higher fuel prices to improve "efficiency." The result? Massive protests, transportation shutdowns, and deepened poverty.

In 2008, as global food prices spiked, Haiti, once a rice-producing nation, faced a hunger crisis. Why? Decades of IMF-enforced trade liberalization had decimated local agriculture in favor of subsidized U.S. imports. Rice farmers abandoned their fields. By the time the loans came, the food was already foreign.

"Debt became a way to punish Haiti for its original sin: daring to be free."
Laurent Dubois, Haiti: The Aftershocks of History (Metropolitan Books, 2012)

Case Study: Mozambique, Loans Without Consent, Crisis Without Escape

Between 2013 and 2016, Mozambique took out over $2 billion in secret loans backed by international banks, intended for infrastructure and maritime security. These debts were hidden from the public and Parliament, yet were later deemed sovereign obligations, meaning the people would pay, no matter who borrowed or why.

When the scandal broke, the IMF suspended its aid program. Foreign investment froze. The currency collapsed. Inflation soared.

To regain favor with the IMF, Mozambique cut spending, raised taxes, and agreed to new austerity measures. Hospitals rationed supplies. Teachers went unpaid. Meanwhile, bankers in London collected fees, and the country's debt soared past 110% of GDP.

No trial was held in Maputo. No banker was extradited. The Mozambican people were sentenced to a generation of repayment.

"The only thing that trickled down was the interest." Mozambican journalist, quoted in The Guardian, 2018

Odious Debt: When the People Pay for the Regime's Corruption

The concept of "odious debt" refers to loans taken out by illegitimate regimes, used not for the public good, but for elite enrichment or repression. Yet under international law, successor governments are still required to repay them.

- Loans given to apartheid-era South Africa were used to build prisons and suppress Black resistance.
- IMF funds lent to dictators like Mobutu Sese Seko of Zaire were stolen or squandered.
- Military regimes in Argentina borrowed billions, then left the tab for future democracies.

These are not debts. They are **instruments of external control**, issued with the knowledge that the borrowers were corrupt, and the citizens would be too poor to resist.

The Illusion of Graduation

The IMF often speaks of "graduation", the point at which a country no longer needs its help. The truth is that **very few countries ever graduate**. They exit one program and enter another. They switch from IMF surveillance to World Bank development lending, or from concessional loans to commercial borrowing, often still guaranteed by international institutions.

Even "debt relief" under programs like HIPC (Heavily Indebted Poor Countries) comes with strings attached: reform your economy, adopt SAP-style policies, and only then will some of your debt be forgiven.

It's like asking a starving man to run a marathon before offering him bread.

Conclusion: Debt as Diplomacy, or Debt as Discipline?

In the 21st century, no tanks are needed to invade a country. Just an interest rate hike. A credit rating downgrade. A funding suspension.

Through debt, the IMF and World Bank have built **a global architecture of obedience,** where nations may be politically independent, but economically subordinated; where parliaments pass budgets approved by invisible hands, where elections change leaders, but not lenders.

Until the structure of international finance changes, "development" will remain conditional, and democracy will always come with an asterisk.

Works Cited (MLA)

Dubois, Laurent. Haiti: The Aftershocks of History. Metropolitan Books, 2012.

Hickel, Jason. The Divide: Global Inequality from Conquest to Free Markets. W.W. Norton, 2017.

Toussaint, Eric. The World Bank: A Critical Primer. Pluto Press, 2008.

The Guardian. "Mozambique's Secret $2bn Debt Deals." The Guardian, 2018.

Stiglitz, Joseph E. Globalization and Its Discontents. W.W. Norton, 2002.

Section IV: Who Really Decides? Voting Shares and Veto Power

How Global Governance Was Designed to Serve the Few While Demanding Consent from the Many

Walk into any IMF or World Bank annual meeting, and you'll be greeted with the iconography of inclusion, flags from around the world, smiling delegations, press briefings where phrases like "multilateral cooperation" and "shared prosperity" dominate the air. On paper, every country has a seat. Every country has a voice. Every country has a vote.

In practice, some voices are louder than others. And some votes matter more than most.

The governance structure of both the International Monetary Fund and the World Bank is **not one-member-one-vote**, as you might expect in a democratic institution. Instead, voting power is tied to **financial contributions**, known as "quotas." The more money a country commits to the institution, the more votes it gets.

Which means in the so-called community of nations, money talks, and it speaks with an American accent.

The Unequal Weight of Votes

As of 2025, the United States holds approximately **16.5%** of voting power in the IMF. That might not sound like a majority, but here's the trick: **any major decision at the IMF requires an 85% supermajority**. This gives the U.S. an **effective veto** over all significant policy changes, including amendments to the Articles of Agreement and decisions on quota reforms.

In other words, **no major action can happen without U.S. approval**, a privilege no other country possesses.

At the World Bank, the voting disparity is nearly stark. High-income countries, primarily in North America and Western Europe, control the bulk of the decision-making power. Meanwhile, **entire continents, such**

as Africa and South America, are relegated to symbolic influence, despite being the primary recipients of World Bank lending and policy interventions.

"This is not multilateralism, it's financial gerrymandering," noted economist Richard Peet in Unholy Trinity (Zed Books, 2009).

The Numbers Behind the Inequality

Let the numbers speak for themselves:

- The **United States** holds ~16.5% of the IMF's voting power
- **Japan**: ~6.1%
- **China**: ~6.0% (despite having the world's largest population)
- The **entire African continent** (54 nations): ~6.8% combined
- The **Caribbean region**: less than 1%

This means that a small group of industrialized nations can **consistently outvote** the very countries most affected by the institutions' policies.

And even when developing nations form coalitions, their collective bargaining power is undercut by **internal divisions**, disparate economic interests, and the ever-present threat of aid suspension or credit downgrade.

The Veto That Shapes the World

Consider this: the United States has used its de facto veto to **block proposals** that would:

- Expand voting power for emerging economies
- Increase funding to low-income countries without additional conditionalities
- Reform debt sustainability metrics to include health and education spending
- Place climate mitigation at the core of lending criteria

Large coalitions of countries in the Global South supported all these efforts. The U.S., backed by a handful of allies, shut them down. Not by force. Not by debate. By **procedure**.

This is not an institution governed by consensus – the capital governs it. In a world where power has long been hoarded, capital still flows in familiar directions.

The "Gentlemen's Agreement"

Since their founding, the IMF and World Bank have also operated under an unwritten rule known as the **"gentlemen's agreement"**: the **head of the IMF is always a European**, while the **head of the World Bank is always an American**.

This backroom deal, born out of post-World War II geopolitics, has persisted for nearly 80 years, regardless of shifts in global economic weight or calls for reform.

Not one African, Asian, or Latin American has ever led these institutions, not because of a lack of qualified candidates, but because **global leadership remains a private club, guarded by legacy and leverage**.

"This arrangement isn't just outdated, it's undemocratic. It institutionalizes exclusion at the highest level of global finance," says Amadou Sy, former Director at the Africa Growth Initiative (Brookings, 2021).

The Consequences of Power Imbalance

When decisions are made by a minority but enforced upon the majority, the result is not cooperation; it is compliance. This imbalance has tangible consequences:

- Loan conditions are crafted to reflect creditor priorities, not local realities
- Policy advice ignores cultural, social, and historical context

- Development benchmarks prioritize macroeconomic indicators over human well-being
- Reform discussions focus on fiscal metrics, not food prices or housing access

Most dangerously, these decisions are made without **meaningful consultation or consent** from the populations they affect.

If a nation were to design its economic plan without public input, it would be called autocratic. When the IMF does it for 80 countries simultaneously, it's called "technical assistance."

Conclusion: Who Decides the Rules of Reform?

The truth is simple: **those who hold the purse strings shape the priorities**. The IMF and World Bank present themselves as arbiters of global stability, but their governance structures betray that promise. In their halls, democracy is not absent; it is inverted.

Those with the least at stake wield the most power. Those who are most impacted hold the smallest voice.

Until these institutions are restructured, not just in rhetoric but in representation, the dream of an equitable global economy will remain just that: a dream.

If democracy is to be global, then global governance must begin by leveling the ground on which decisions are made. Without that, every "vote" is just a performance, and every policy, a reflection of the empire that never truly ended.

Works Cited (MLA)

Peet, Richard. Unholy Trinity: The IMF, World Bank, and WTO. Zed Books, 2009.

Hickel, Jason. The Divide: Global Inequality from Conquest to Free Markets. W.W. Norton, 2017.

Sy, Amadou. "Reforming Global Financial Governance." Brookings Institution, 2021.

Stiglitz, Joseph E. Globalization and Its Discontents Revisited. W.W. Norton & Company, 2018.

Toussaint, Eric. The World Bank: A Critical Primer. Pluto Press, 2008.

Section V: Privatization and the Selling of the State

How Public Goods Became Profit Centers, And Sovereignty Was Lost One Utility at a Time

The rhetoric was always the same: "efficiency," "modernization," "free markets." Behind the slogans of reform lay a more troubling reality, **the systematic dismantling of the state**, piece by piece, sector by sector. Schools, clinics, water pipes, electrical grids, and agricultural cooperatives, none were spared. All were rebranded as "inefficient," "corrupt," or "too expensive."

What is the solution offered by the IMF and World Bank? **Privatization**.

What they proposed was simple in theory: governments should not be in the business of running services. The private sector, they argued, could deliver better outcomes at lower costs, with greater innovation and less waste.

However, in the Global South, this theory often fell short of reality. Privatization did not create accountability. It **created monopolies**, foreign-owned, profit-driven, and structurally insulated from democratic oversight.

The result was a new form of colonization: not by flags or armies, but by corporations and contracts. And the victims, as always, were the poor.

The IMF Playbook: Liquidate to Stabilize

Privatization became a core conditionality in structural adjustment programs. Countries were told that to access loans or to qualify for debt forgiveness, they had to sell off public assets:

- Water utilities
- Power companies
- Telecommunications
- Banks
- Mining operations
- Ports and transport systems

These assets were often sold at fire-sale prices to multinational corporations. The rationale? These sales would reduce fiscal deficits and increase investor confidence. The reality was a massive transfer of national wealth into private hands, often foreign, and frequently unaccountable.

Case Study 1: Bolivia, The Cochabamba Water Revolt

In 1999, the World Bank advised Bolivia to privatize its water system in Cochabamba, a major city already struggling with poverty. The contract was awarded to Aguas del Tunari, a consortium led by the U.S. corporation Bechtel.

Immediately, water prices soared, doubling or tripling for many families. Worse, the company sought to control **all sources of water** in the region, including **rainwater**. It became illegal to collect rain in barrels. Those who did faced fines or jail.

What followed was a rebellion.

Protests swept the city. Students, farmers, and workers united under the banner: "Water is life, it is not for sale." The government declared martial law. Police fired live rounds into crowds. Dozens were injured. A 17-year-old boy, Víctor Hugo Daza, was shot and killed.

Eventually, the government was forced to terminate the contract and expel the company. Bechtel later sued Bolivia for $50 million through a secretive international arbitration court. The suit was eventually dropped, but the message was clear: even when people win, corporations don't back down easily.

"Privatization was supposed to bring water to everyone. Instead, it brought war." Oscar Olivera, protest leader and author of Cochabamba! Water War in Bolivia (South End Press, 2004)

Case Study 2: Tanzania, A Pipeline to Nowhere

In the early 2000s, the World Bank pressured Tanzania to privatize its electricity utility, TANESCO, as part of a structural adjustment program. The British company Biwater was brought in through a subsidiary called City Water Services.

What followed was chaos:

- Water supply decreased
- Infrastructure deteriorated
- Biwater failed to meet contractual obligations

Within two years, the Tanzanian government canceled the contract. Biwater responded by suing Tanzania at the International Centre for Settlement of Investment Disputes (ICSID), demanding compensation for lost profits.

Tanzania had to spend years and millions defending itself, not for failing to honor a fair contract, but for **reclaiming sovereignty over a failed deal**.

"We were told to trust the market. The market never came. Only the bills did. Tanzanian civil society leader, quoted in Water Justice (Bakker et al., 2012)

The Broader Pattern: Austerity Meets Extraction

In many other countries, privatization unfolded with the same brutal logic:

- **Ghana**: Electricity rates surged after privatization, leading to mass protests and a national campaign called "Dumsor Must Stop" (referring to rolling blackouts).
- **South Africa**: Water privatization in poor townships led to disconnections for those who couldn't pay, fueling anger and civil unrest.
- **India**: The privatization of public hospitals under state reforms forced millions of poor patients into debt or death.
- **Nigeria**: The telecom sector became profitable, **but foreign-owned**, with repatriated profits and little reinvestment in rural infrastructure.

The irony was suffocating in the name of efficiency; vital services became **less accessible**. In the name of "modernization," countries auctioned off their future.

And yet, in the World Bank's publications, this was heralded as progress.

Privatization Without Accountability

What made these deals even more dangerous was the **lack of oversight**. Contracts were often negotiated in secret. Public opinion was ignored. Labor unions were crushed or excluded. And when things went wrong, governments, not corporations, bore the political fallout.

Most privatized services operated as **monopolies**, with no competition and no incentive to serve the public interest. Worse, many were protected by **bilateral investment treaties**, allowing them to sue governments for attempting to regulate prices or revoke licenses.

This was not capitalism. It was conquest, disguised in the spreadsheets of economists and the memos of mission chiefs.

Conclusion: The Price of Selling the State

Privatization was not just an economic policy. It was a **political project**, a systematic effort to shrink the role of the state, not by vote or debate, but by decree from above. It replaced public control with private extraction. It replaced accountability with arbitration courts. And it replaced the idea of service with the logic of profit.

For many in the Global South, the question is no longer whether privatization "worked." The question is: **who did it work for?**

Until nations can reclaim their right to own, manage, and distribute public goods without fear of financial retaliation, there can be no true development. And certainly, no democracy.

Because a democracy where you can vote for leaders, but not for water, is a democracy in name only.

Works Cited (MLA)

Bakker, Karen, et al. Water Justice. MIT Press, 2012.Olivera, Oscar.

Cochabamba! Water War in Bolivia. South End Press, 2004.

Peet, Richard. Unholy Trinity: The IMF, World Bank, and WTO. Zed Books, 2009.

Toussaint, Eric. The World Bank: A Critical Primer. Pluto Press, 2008.

Hickel, Jason. The Divide: Global Inequality from Conquest to Free Markets. W.W. Norton, 2017.

Section VI: From Austerity to "Good Governance", The Language Evolves

Rebranding Empire: When Discipline Is Sold as Dialogue

Language is not neutral. In the realm of international finance, it has always been a weapon, sharp, strategic, and shrouded in diplomacy. And over the past four decades, as opposition to structural adjustment deepened, the IMF and World Bank did not abandon their core doctrines. They **rebranded them**.

The words changed. The power remained.

Where they once spoke of "austerity," they now speak of "fiscal responsibility." Where "conditionality" was once overt, we now hear "policy dialogue." "Liberalization" has become "investment climate reform." "Privatization" is cloaked as "public-private partnerships." And most critically, a new buzzword emerged to justify continued oversight: **"good governance."**

On the surface, it sounds noble. Who could be against good governance? Beneath the veneer lies an evolving strategy of control, one that abandons the stick of the 1980s for the velvet glove of technocracy.

The Rise of the Poverty Reduction Strategy Paper (PRSP)

By the late 1990s, the IMF and World Bank faced growing resistance. From anti-globalization protests in Seattle to revolts in Cochabamba and Accra, the costs of SAPs were no longer hidden. Activists exposed the human toll. Academics challenged economics. Even some former insiders' broke ranks.

In response, the institutions initiated a new approach: the **Poverty Reduction Strategy Paper (PRSP), a document** that countries had to prepare, in collaboration with civil society, to qualify for debt relief under the Heavily Indebted Poor Countries (HIPC) Initiative.

At first glance, it seemed like a sea change: the poor were being asked to help design their futures. In practice, the PRSPs often **replicated old frameworks**, written by consultants, guided by preset templates, and measured by macroeconomic targets. Participation was often superficial. "Consultation" amounted to a few workshops with NGOs. The final drafts still had to be approved by IMF and World Bank staff.

"The PRSP process was participatory on their terms. We got to speak, but not to decide."
Ghanaian civil society leader, Third World Quarterly, 2005

The core message remained: to assess relief, you must conform even if it's now dressed in the language of empowerment.

Good Governance: A Trojan Horse of Technocracy

"Good governance" entered the development lexicon in the 1990s. It emphasized transparency, accountability, anti-corruption, and institutional capacity.

Again, all good things. Who defines them? Who decides what counts as "corruption" or "capacity"?

In practice, good governance became a **gatekeeping tool**. Countries were rated, ranked, and monitored. Those who scored well received grants and favorable loans. Those who didn't were punished, not by vote, but by spreadsheet.

More troubling, governance metrics often ignore **historical context**. They judged post-colonial states by Western bureaucratic norms, without accounting for the structural violence of colonialism, the social legitimacy of customary systems, or the lived reality of hybrid governance.

And most paradoxically, **the same institutions that had enabled dictatorships for decades now demanded democratic performance**. The IMF, which had loaned billions to autocrats like Mobutu and Pinochet, now lectured elected governments about transparency.

"It's like being told how to manage your home by the very person who looted it." Tanzanian scholar and former finance minister, 2016

The Myth of Local Ownership

Another buzzword that gained traction in the 2000s was **"country ownership."** IMF and World Bank officials began claiming that reforms were no longer imposed; they were "homegrown."

"Ownership" meant something else: if a policy failed, the blame shifted **from the lender to the borrower**. The script had been flipped. Austerity was still being enforced, but now the accountability lay with national governments.

This rhetorical shift allowed the Bretton Woods institutions to continue dictating economic policy, while appearing to stand at arm's length.

Case Study: Rwanda, A Model of Technocratic Discipline

Rwanda has often been held up as a "success story" of the post-PRSP era. The World Bank praised its reforms. The IMF celebrated its fiscal discipline. The country climbed the Doing Business rankings.

Beneath the surface, the picture was more complex.

- Poverty reduction was absolute, but uneven.
- Health and education improved, but mainly through donor dependence.
- Political dissent was tightly controlled.
- Civil society's participation in economic planning was limited.

The model worked for donors. It delivered measurable outputs. It also deepened a form of technocratic governance where policy was crafted to please creditors, not necessarily citizens.

"We are taught to manage the economy, not to ask who it serves." Rwandan development planner, confidential interview, 2022

Conclusion: Language as Leverage

Today, the IMF and World Bank rarely mention "structural adjustment." They avoid the word "austerity." The **logic remains unchanged**: discipline your economy, or face isolation. Cut deficits before cutting inequality. Listen to markets before listening to your people.

The language has softened, but the power it protects has not.

Until governance is defined not by external indicators but by internal legitimacy, by the ability of a society to determine its path, the shift from austerity to "good governance" will remain a rebranding, not a reckoning.

And the Global South will continue to be spoken to, written about, and judged, without truly being heard.

Works Cited (MLA)

Craig, David, and Doug Porter. Development Beyond Neoliberalism? Governance, Poverty Reduction and Political Economy. Routledge, 2006.

Harrison, Graham. The World Bank and Africa: The Construction of Governance States. Routledge, 2004.

Peet, Richard. Unholy Trinity: The IMF, World Bank, and WTO. Zed Books, 2009.

World Bank. Rwanda: Rebuilding an Effective State. World Bank Publications, 2011.

Stiglitz, Joseph E. Globalization and Its Discontents Revisited. W.W. Norton, 2018.

Section VII: Resistance and Reclamation

The Global South Is No Longer Asking: It's Rewriting the Rules

For decades, it seemed inevitable. The IMF and World Bank would dictate, and nations would obey. Ministers would nod solemnly at press conferences. Presidents would smile beside officials from Washington and Brussels. Protesters would be ignored. Alternatives dismissed. And debt, always the debt, would hang like a noose.

The world has changed.

Slowly, sometimes painfully, and often against all odds, the Global South is pushing back, not just through protests, but through policy changes, not only with marches, but with alternatives. A new generation of leaders, economists, and movements are rising, not to beg for reform but to demand accountability. And in some cases, to build new financial futures that do not start with surrender.

This is a story of resistance. Not just a moment, but a movement.

Argentina: Default as Defiance

In 2001, Argentina did what was once unthinkable: it defaulted on $95 billion in sovereign debt, the largest default in world history at the time. Years of IMF-imposed austerity had devastated the country: unemployment surged, pensions were gutted, and suicide rates rose.

When the peso collapsed, the people rose up. They banged pots in the streets, stormed banks, and chanted: "¡Que se vayan todos!", "They all must go."

The government fell. And in the chaos, Argentina walked away from the IMF.

The pundits predicted disaster. Instead, Argentina's economy recovered. From 2003 to 2007, under President Néstor Kirchner, the country saw 8% annual GDP growth. Poverty and inequality decreased. Public investment resumed.

In 2006, Kirchner paid off the IMF in full, **not as a sign of loyalty, but as a declaration of independence**.

"We will never again be subjected to policies that bring us to our knees," he declared boldly to Congress.

Ecuador: Debt on Trial

Under President Rafael Correa, Ecuador took a bold step: it publicly **audited its national debt** with participation from civil society, economists, and legal scholars.

The audit revealed that much of the debt, especially from the 1980s and 1990s, was **illegitimate**, contracted by military regimes without democratic consent and often under corrupt terms.

In 2008, Ecuador announced it would default on portions of that debt. Creditors howled. Credit ratings plummeted. The government stood firm.

In time, Ecuador restructured its bonds on **far more favorable terms,** saving billions in interest payments and proving that moral arguments, when backed by political will, could yield material gains.

This wasn't chaos. It was sovereignty reclaimed.

Bolivia: Water Is a Right, not a Commodity

Following the 2000 Cochabamba Water War, Bolivia's political trajectory shifted dramatically. In 2005, Evo Morales, a former coca farmer and indigenous leader, was elected president. His platform? Reverse the privatizations. Reclaim national resources. Rebuild the state.

His government renegotiated contracts with multinational gas and mining companies. It increased royalties. It re-nationalized key sectors.

Despite intense pressure from international financial institutions, Bolivia saw **steady economic growth**, poverty reduction, and a dramatic expansion of public health and education.

Morales made it clear: **development doesn't require surrendering control**.

Africa's Awakening: Toward a Sovereign Financial Future

Across Africa, resistance has taken root in new forms:

- The **African Union** has called for the establishment of a **Pan-African Monetary Fund** to reduce dependence on the IMF.
- Nations like **Ghana**, **Kenya**, and **Nigeria** are increasingly turning to **domestic debt markets** and **regional development banks**.

- Leaders like **Thomas Sankara**, though assassinated for their defiance, remain icons of the demand for economic self-determination.

In 2022, **Zambia** became the first African nation to default under the COVID-era debt crisis. Unlike in the past, civil society demanded transparency, equity in negotiations, and inclusion of social spending protections.

The narrative has shifted. **The IMF is no longer the only voice in the room**.

The Rise of South–South Solidarity

From the formation of **BRICS** (Brazil, Russia, India, China, South Africa) to the expansion of **regional development banks** like the Asian Infrastructure Investment Bank (AIIB), the world is moving away from a unipolar financial system.

These efforts are not without flaws. They represent a critical break from the belief that development must always be mediated through the IMF and World Bank.

They signal a truth long denied: **the Global South has options, and a memory**.

Conclusion: From Subjects to Architects

This resistance is not about nostalgia or nationalism. It is about justice. For too long, development has meant obedience. Aid has meant silence. Debt has meant discipline.

A new world is emerging, where nations are not mere subjects of policy, but **architects of their futures**.

The IMF and World Bank can no longer count on compliance. The age of quiet suffering is over. What comes next may be messy, uncertain, and contested, but it will be **ours**.

As Kwame Nkrumah once said: “We face neither East nor West. We face forward."

Works Cited (MLA)

Becker, Marc. Ecuador: Correa and the Citizens' Revolution. NACLA Report on the Americas, 2008.Hickel, Jason.

The Divide: Global Inequality from Conquest to Free Markets. W.W. Norton, 2017.

Lopez, Lucia. "Argentina's Economic Recovery: Lessons in Defying the IMF." OpenDemocracy, 2011.

Olivera, Oscar. Cochabamba! Water War in Bolivia. South End Press, 2004.

Toussaint, Eric. Debt, the IMF, and the World Bank: Sixty Questions, Sixty Answers. Monthly Review Press, 2010.

Section VIII: The IMF's New Mandates: Climate, Gender, Inclusion... or Distraction?

When Empires Learn to Speak the Language of Justice

In recent years, something has shifted. The IMF and World Bank, once seen as guardians of market orthodoxy, have begun to speak a new language. They talk of **climate justice**, **gender empowerment**, **inclusive growth**, and **social protection**. Their reports are adorned with photos of women entrepreneurs, children in schools, and solar panels shimmering under the African sun.

They sound less like institutions of discipline and more like partners in progress.

Language, as always, is political. This new rhetoric, though softer, raises a tricky question:

Has the mission changed or just the marketing?

Green Finance or Green Control?

In the face of the mounting climate catastrophe, the World Bank and the IMF now position themselves as champions of climate action. They have pledged billions in climate adaptation, energy transition, and resilience funding. Climate risk assessments are now part of macroeconomic analysis. Carbon markets and "nature-based solutions" are part of development planning.

How are these programs structured?

- Most **climate funds are issued as loans**, not grants, adding to already crushing debt burdens.
- "Green growth" often prioritizes corporate-led investments over community-based solutions.
- Renewable energy contracts are awarded to foreign firms, with profits expatriated, and little local capacity built.
- Land acquisitions for carbon offsets have displaced Indigenous and rural communities in parts of Africa and Southeast Asia.

This is not climate justice. It's **green colonialism**, where the Global South is once again asked to bear the cost of a crisis it did not create, while being denied sovereignty over the response.

"We are asked to adapt but never allowed to control." Ugandan climate activist, COP26 statement

Gender as Conditionality

The IMF has also embraced the language of gender equality. It has published research on how empowering women boosts GDP. It urges governments to invest in female labor force participation, support childcare, and reduce barriers for women entrepreneurs.

These are worthy goals. In practice, **gender inclusion is often instrumentalized,** used not to affirm rights but to justify reforms that serve economic goals.

For example:

- In some countries, women are encouraged to enter the labor force **only to offset public sector job cuts**.

- Microloans are promoted as tools of empowerment, yet many trap women in cycles of debt.
- Gender budgeting reforms are implemented without expanding the fiscal space, forcing ministries to **choose between priorities**, not expand them.

And in the broader context, **gender discourse is rarely accompanied by structural changes** in how trade, debt, and investment rules constrain national policy space.

What results are a dangerous illusion: that justice can be achieved **without power**.

Inclusion Without Transformation

Perhaps the most sweeping change is the institutions' adoption of "inclusive growth" as a core objective. Gone is the language of trickle-down. In its place are phrases like:

- "Leaving no one behind"
- "Human capital investment"
- "Targeted social protection"
- "Digital financial inclusion"

As many critics have noted, inclusion in **what**? Growth **for whom**?

If the underlying development model remains extractive, unequal, and externally dictated, then inclusion becomes **assimilation,** not emancipation. It invites the poor into a system that still privileges capital over community, profit over people.

"We are included only as laborers and borrowers, as decision-makers or rights-holders.", an Indian grassroots organizer, quoted in Development and Change, 2021

Case Study: The IMF in Pakistan's Social Spending Debate

In 2019, the IMF approved a $6 billion bailout for Pakistan, one of dozens in its history. The loan came with conditions: cuts to energy subsidies, increases in regressive taxes, and privatization of state assets.

At the same time, the IMF praised Pakistan for its **Benazir Income Support Program**, a cash transfer initiative aimed at poor women.

The contradiction was glaring. On the one hand, the IMF applauded social protection. On the other hand, its fiscal targets **undermined the very capacity** of the state to fund such programs sustainably.

Pakistan was praised for "inclusive reforms," even as millions faced rising food and fuel costs.

A Smarter Empire Is Still an Empire

Make no mistake: these shifts in language are not meaningless. They reflect real pressure, mobilized by civil society, scholars, feminist economists, climate justice movements, and governments in the Global South.

Without a shift in **power**, these rhetorical changes risk becoming distractions. They dress up old frameworks in progressive clothing. They soften the optics while preserving the architecture.

A smarter empire learns to speak your language, so you lower your guard.

Conclusion: Words Are Not Liberation

We must judge institutions not by what they say, but by what they do, and who they serve.

If climate finance is debt-based, if gender reforms are market-centric, and if inclusion depends on compliance, then we are not witnessing true transformation. Instead, we see adaptation, not by the oppressed, but by the powerful.

True justice demands more than just representation in reports. It demands redistribution. It demands repair. It demands a world where development is not merely offered as charity but reclaimed as a right.

Until then, every press release must be read like a contract, and every kind word weighed against its cost.

Works Cited (MLA)

Hickel, Jason. Less Is More: How Degrowth Will Save the World. Windmill Books, 2020.

Bretton Woods Project. The Gendered Cost of IMF Policies. BrettonWoodsProject.org, 2021.

Development and Change Editorial Board. "Inclusion or Illusion? Rethinking Development Targets." Development and Change, vol. 52, no. 2, 2021.

World Bank. Climate Change Action Plan 2021–2025. World Bank Publications, 2021.

Oxfam International. Climate Finance Shadow Report 2023. Oxfam.org, 2023.

Section IX: Conclusion: Who Owes Whom?

The Global South Has Paid in Blood, Resources, and Silence

Let us now ask the question that rarely makes it into economic forecasts, IMF briefings, or World Bank reports:

Who really owes whom?

For over half a century, the Global South has been portrayed as indebted, unstable, and irresponsible. It has been told repeatedly that salvation lies in loans, that wisdom lives in Washington, and that governance means surrendering control to the same institutions that once funded dictators, imposed austerity, and drained public wealth into private coffers.

The balance sheet of history tells a different story.

If debt is the measure of moral obligation, then the Global South is not a debtor; it is a creditor. It is owed reparations, not reforms.

The Real Costs Hidden in the Fine Print

What is the value of forests razed to meet debt payments? What is the price of teachers laid off so that balance sheets align with IMF targets?
What is the cost of a generation of African, Asian, and Latin American youth born into states too poor to protect them, **not because the wealth didn't exist, but because it was exported**?

For decades, the South has paid with:

- **Its land** was seized or privatized under pressure
- **Its labor** was cheapened for global supply chains
- **Its dignity** was traded for access to capital
- **Its sovereignty** was sacrificed to conditionality

And yet it is still labeled the one in debt.

This inversion is not economic. It is political. It is colonial logic in financial form.

Debt as Discipline, Not Development

The IMF and World Bank were never neutral. They are political actors in economic clothing, servants of a global order that values "stability" more than justice, and GDP growth more than equitable well-being.

They call it assistance, but it is **governance without accountability**.

They call it cooperation, but it is a **hierarchy without consent**.

And still, the people rise. They audit their debts. They protest on their terms. They build cooperatives, regional alliances, and new financial institutions. They refuse to be spoken to. They **demand to speak back**.

The Reckoning Ahead

To imagine a world beyond these shackles, we must first speak plainly:

- Canceling unjust debt is not radical; it is restitution.
- Reclaiming public services is not inefficiency; it is sovereignty.
- Investing in people before markets is not populism, it is justice.

The question is not whether the IMF and World Bank can be reformed. It is whether **development can exist without domination**.

Because until the world begins with that truth, every dollar lent will carry an invisible chain. Every loan disbursed will echo not with freedom, but with **the sound of a lion's growl, softened only by better marketing**.

The jungle remembers; the gazelles have stopped running.

Works Cited (MLA)

Hickel, Jason. The Divide: Global Inequality from Conquest to Free Markets. W.W. Norton, 2017.

Toussaint, Eric. Debt, the IMF, and the World Bank: Sixty Questions, Sixty Answers. Monthly Review Press, 2010.

Stiglitz, Joseph E. Globalization and Its Discontents Revisited. W.W. Norton, 2018.

Oxfam International. False Promises: How the IMF Fails the Poor. Oxfam Briefing Paper, 2020.

Bretton Woods Project. The Hidden Costs of Debt. BrettonWoodsProject.org, 2023.

References:

Bakker, Karen, et al. *Water Justice*. MIT Press, 2012.

Becker, Marc. *Ecuador: Correa and the Citizens' Revolution*. NACLA Report on the Americas, 2008.

Bond, Patrick. *Looting Africa: The Economics of Exploitation*. Zed Books, 2006.

Craig, David, and Doug Porter. *Development Beyond Neoliberalism? Governance, Poverty Reduction and Political Economy*. Routledge, 2006.

Dubois, Laurent. *Haiti: The Aftershocks of History*. Metropolitan Books, 2012.

Harrison, Graham. *The World Bank and Africa: The Construction of Governance States*. Routledge, 2004.

Hickel, Jason. *The Divide: Global Inequality from Conquest to Free Markets*. W.W. Norton, 2017.

Hickel, Jason. *Less Is More: How Degrowth Will Save the World*. Windmill Books, 2020.

Lopez, Lucia. "Argentina's Economic Recovery: Lessons in Defying the IMF." *OpenDemocracy*, 2011.

Olivera, Oscar. *Cochabamba! Water War in Bolivia*. South End Press, 2004.

Peet, Richard. *Unholy Trinity: The IMF, World Bank and WTO*. Zed Books, 2009.

Stiglitz, Joseph E. *Globalization and Its Discontents*. W.W. Norton & Company, 2002.

Stiglitz, Joseph E. *Globalization and Its Discontents Revisited*. W.W. Norton & Company, 2018.

Toussaint, Eric. *The World Bank: A Critical Primer*. Pluto Press,

2008.

Toussaint, Eric. *Debt, the IMF, and the World Bank: Sixty Questions, Sixty Answers*. Monthly Review Press, 2010.

World Bank. *Climate Change Action Plan 2021–2025*. World Bank Publications, 2021.

Glossary

Austerity: Economic policies implemented to reduce government deficits, often through spending cuts and tax increases.

Bretton Woods Conference: The 1944 meeting that established the IMF and World Bank, shaping the global financial system post-WWII.

Conditionalities: Economic policy requirements imposed by international financial institutions as conditions for receiving loans or aid.

Debt Trap: A situation in which a country is forced to borrow more to service existing debt, leading to a cycle of dependency.

Democracy, export of: The promotion of democratic systems and institutions abroad, often influenced by geopolitical interests.

Development Finance: Financial resources and mechanisms aimed at supporting economic development in low- and middle-income countries.

Ghana, SAPs in: Implementation of Structural Adjustment Programs in Ghana during the 1980s and 1990s under IMF/World Bank guidance.

IMF: The International Monetary Fund, an international financial institution that provides monetary cooperation and financial stability.

Neoliberalism: A political-economic philosophy favoring free-market capitalism, deregulation, and reduction in government spending.

Privatization: The transfer of ownership of state-owned enterprises to private entities.

SAPs (Structural Adjustment Programs): Economic reforms imposed by the IMF and World Bank, typically involving austerity, deregulation, and privatization.

Sovereignty: The authority of a state to govern itself without external interference.

World Bank: An international financial institution that provides loans and grants to the governments of poorer countries for development projects.

Colonialism: The policy or practice of acquiring political control over another country, occupying it with settlers, and exploiting it economically.

Digital Colonialism: The control and exploitation of digital resources and infrastructure in the Global South by powerful tech companies or states.

Surveillance Capitalism: A market form that relies on collecting and selling data extracted from people's online behavior.

Weaponized Democracy: The use of democratic rhetoric or institutions as tools for achieving strategic or ideological objectives, often abroad.

Selected Bibliography

Academic Books and Articles

Chomsky, Noam. (1999). The New Military Humanism: Lessons from Kosovo. Monroe, ME: Common Courage Press.

Fanon, Frantz. (1963). The Wretched of the Earth. New York: Grove Press.

Fukuyama, Francis. (2006). After the Neocons: America at the Crossroads. New Haven: Yale University Press.

Hochschild, Adam. (1998). King Leopold's Ghost. New York: Houghton Mifflin.

Klein, Naomi. (2007). The Shock Doctrine: The Rise of Disaster Capitalism. New York: Picador.

Mamdani, Mahmood. (2004). Good Muslim, Bad Muslim: America, the Cold War, and the Roots of Terror. New York: Pantheon Books.

Piketty, Thomas. (2014). Capital in the Twenty-First Century. Cambridge: Harvard University Press.

Sachs, Jeffrey. (2005). The End of Poverty: Economic Possibilities for Our Time. New York: Penguin Books.

Stiglitz, Joseph. (2002). Globalization and Its Discontents. New York: W.W. Norton & Company.

Podcasts, Videos, and Documentaries

Al Jazeera. (2016). The Lobby (Documentary Series).

Democracy Now! (Various Episodes). https://www.democracynow.org

The Intercept. (2021). Deconstructed Podcast.

Vice News. (2018). Libya: The Aftermath of NATO Intervention (Video).

The New York Times: The Daily. (Various Episodes). https://www.nytimes.com/column/the-daily

Websites and Digital Sources

IMF. (2024). www.imf.org

World Bank. (2024). www.worldbank.org

Transparency International. (2024). www.transparency.org

United Nations. (2024). www.un.org

African Union. (2024). www.au.int

The Guardian. (2024). www.theguardian.com

Foreign Policy. (2024). www.foreignpolicy.com

Official Documents and Reports

African Union. (2015). Agenda 2063: The Africa We Want. Addis Ababa: African Union Commission.

International Monetary Fund. (2022). World Economic Outlook: War Sets Back the Global Recovery. Washington, DC: IMF.

United Nations. (2005). 2005 World Summit Outcome. UN General Assembly Document A/RES/60/1.

United Nations. (2011). Report of the International Commission on Intervention and State Sovereignty: The Responsibility to Protect.

World Bank. (2021). World Development Report 2021: Data for Better Lives. Washington, DC: The World Bank.

World Bank. (2023). International Debt Statistics 2023. Washington, DC: The World Bank.

United Nations Economic Commission for Africa. (2019). Governing Data for Africa's Transformation. Addis Ababa: UNECA.

Transparency International. (2022). Corruption Perceptions Index 2022.

UN Human Rights Council. (2021). Impact of Sanctions on Human

Rights. A/HRC/48/28.

South African Truth and Reconciliation Commission. (1998). Final Report. Government of South Africa.

Selected Bibliography

Academic Books and Articles

Chomsky, Noam. (1999). The New Military Humanism: Lessons from Kosovo. Monroe, ME: Common Courage Press.

Fanon, Frantz. (1963). The Wretched of the Earth. New York: Grove Press.

Fukuyama, Francis. (2006). After the Neocons: America at the Crossroads. New Haven: Yale University Press.

Hochschild, Adam. (1998). King Leopold's Ghost. New York: Houghton Mifflin.

Klein, Naomi. (2007). The Shock Doctrine: The Rise of Disaster Capitalism. New York: Picador.

Mamdani, Mahmood. (2004). Good Muslim, Bad Muslim: America, the Cold War, and the Roots of Terror. New York: Pantheon Books.

Piketty, Thomas. (2014). Capital in the Twenty-First Century. Cambridge: Harvard University Press.

Sachs, Jeffrey. (2005). The End of Poverty: Economic Possibilities for Our Time. New York: Penguin Books.

Stiglitz, Joseph. (2002). Globalization and Its Discontents. New York: W.W. Norton & Company.

Podcasts, Videos, and Documentaries

Al Jazeera. (2016). The Lobby (Documentary Series).

Democracy Now! (Various Episodes). https://www.democracynow.org

The Intercept. (2021). Deconstructed Podcast.

Vice News. (2018). Libya: The Aftermath of NATO Intervention (Video).

The New York Times: The Daily. (Various Episodes). https://www.nytimes.com/column/the-daily

Websites and Digital Sources

IMF. (2024). www.imf.org

World Bank. (2024). www.worldbank.org

Transparency International. (2024). www.transparency.org

United Nations. (2024). www.un.org

African Union. (2024). www.au.int

The Guardian. (2024). www.theguardian.com

Foreign Policy. (2024). www.foreignpolicy.com

Official Documents and Reports

African Union. (2015). Agenda 2063: The Africa We Want. Addis Ababa: African Union Commission.

International Monetary Fund. (2022). World Economic Outlook: War Sets Back the Global Recovery. Washington, DC: IMF.

United Nations. (2005). 2005 World Summit Outcome. UN General Assembly Document A/RES/60/1.

United Nations. (2011). Report of the International Commission on Intervention and State Sovereignty: The Responsibility to Protect.

World Bank. (2021). World Development Report 2021: Data for Better Lives. Washington, DC: The World Bank.

World Bank. (2023). International Debt Statistics 2023. Washington, DC: The World Bank.

United Nations Economic Commission for Africa. (2019). Governing Data for Africa's Transformation. Addis Ababa: UNECA.

Transparency International. (2022). Corruption Perceptions Index 2022.

UN Human Rights Council. (2021). Impact of Sanctions on Human Rights. A/HRC/48/28.

South African Truth and Reconciliation Commission. (1998). Final Report. Government of South Africa.

Index

www.ingramcontent.com/pod-product-compliance
Lightning Source LLC
Chambersburg PA
CBHW062124020426
42335CB00013B/1092

* 9 7 8 1 9 6 7 6 2 3 6 9 3 *